D0523744

CATHOLICISM
A Complete Introduction

Teach Yourself®

CATHOLICISM
A Complete Introduction

Peter Stanford

Also available in ebook

Contents

Foreword

I thought long and hard when Peter asked me to write a few words as an introduction to this book. It was not that I was reticent about helping an old friend, or that I feared he might not be up to the task of explaining Catholicism. It's just that I could think of so many people more qualified for the task than me.

I have been a practising Catholic all my life. It remains an important part of who I am. But I certainly would never consider myself an expert.

There is no doubt that this book is timely. Faith and religion, for good and not-so-good reasons, are very much back on the public agenda. This makes it more important than ever that discussions are based on the facts rather than fiction, which is, sadly, not always the case.

It is giving the facts in a fair and balanced way that has been Peter's goal with this book about Catholicism. He believes, as I do, that going back to the basics in this way will promote understanding and tolerance, and help, too, to highlight the fundamental and decent values that our great religions share.

I hope you find the book as informative and interesting as I did.

Cherie Booth, QC

Introduction

There are an estimated 1.229 billion Catholics around the world today. In theory, and in the rhetoric of the Church, all accept the *magisterium* (teaching authority) of its leader, the Pope, the successor to the Apostle Peter, and all accept the teachings of the Church, set out most clearly in the *Catechism of the Catholic Church*, a rulebook reintroduced in the 1990s by Pope John Paul II.

Yet the *Catechism*'s 700 pages and almost 3,000 entries, detailing what Catholics can and cannot do, think or believe, do not tell the story of Catholicism. Neither does a careful reading of 2,000 years of papal pronouncements. For the Church is not and never has been a monolith, filled with automatons who simply do as they are told. It is a human institution and so there are almost as many interpretations of what it is to be Catholic today as there are Catholics.

Individual believers choose the areas of Church teaching where they place the greatest emphasis. This may be on its social teaching (for example, demanding a more equal playing field between rich and poor nations); on the format of the Catholic liturgy; or on Catholic approaches to such vexed subjects as abortion, in vitro fertilization and sexual morality. There are only two constants. One, each personal formulation of what precisely it means to be a Catholic will differ from the next, and, two, you will never find a Catholic who believes that each and every teaching of their Church is universally marvellous and absolutely spot on.

I say that on the basis of having spent three decades as a 'professional' Catholic, mixing in the course of my work with believers around the world, and more like half a century as a 'private' Catholic, trying and often failing to live out the Church's teaching.

I was brought up in that bastion of English Catholicism, Liverpool. After university, I had no particular idea of what

I wanted to do – certainly no vocation – but pitched up as a journalist at first the *Tablet*, the international Catholic weekly, and then the *Catholic Herald*, next a weekly broadsheet serving English, Welsh and Irish Catholics. For four years until 1992 I was editor of the latter. Since then I have covered Catholicism in particular and religion in general among the many other topics that I have tackled in newspapers, magazines, television and radio programmes and a series of books.

The thing that continues to enthral me about the Church is the ties that hold Catholics to it, arguably over and above those that bind people brought up in other faiths to their particular denomination. You don't, for instance, meet many lapsed Lutherans and Methodists, but with cradle Catholics, even when as adults they struggle with many of the Church's beliefs and practices, there remains a residual and lifelong connection. Part of what it is to be Catholic – alongside the more obvious matter of a relationship with God – is navigating a relationship with the institution of the Church. That is what unites the 1.229 billion Catholics worldwide, and is the subject of this book.

Peculiar to Catholicism, too, is the figure of the Pope. An institution that has endured for 2,000 years shouldn't in theory change every time someone new is in charge, but certainly my experience of the last three popes – the force of nature that was John Paul II, the retiring wise uncle that was Benedict XVI, and now the beguiling, smiling, informal, headline-grabbing Francis – has been that the atmosphere within the Catholic Church alters in each pontificate. Sometimes it is subtle – Benedict had, after all, served for many years as John Paul's right-hand man – but other times it is as if every certainty is suddenly capable of radical new interpretation. That is the impact Pope Francis is having on the Church. No one quite knows where the hopes and expectations he has unleashed will eventually lead, but everyone in the pews wants to be there for the ride.

To Catholics of my generation (I was born in 1961), the idea that you could teach yourself Catholicism is, at first glance, a difficult one. We were brought up to believe that, if you had any questions about your faith, you should turn to a priest. The world – including the Catholic one – has moved on from those times, as my children never cease to remind me, but I have still found myself, in writing this, turning to priests and theologians for advice and guidance on key questions of doctrine. I would like to thank in particular Fathers Shaun Middleton, John Hemer and Stephen McBrearty for all their guidance in this project.

All biblical quotations are from the *New Jerusalem Bible*, published by Darton, Longman & Todd. Quotations from the *Catechism of the Catholic Church* come from the Revised Edition published by Geoffrey Chapman.

Peter Stanford, London, 2015

Part One

Catholicism – the basics

What is Catholicism?

In this chapter you will learn:

▶ *about the key role of the Pope within Catholicism*

▶ *why Catholics are different from other Christians*

▶ *how today's Catholic Church regards other faiths.*

The oldest institution in the Western world

The Catholic Church is the oldest institution in the Western world. Its history can be traced back over 2,000 years to the life and times of Jesus Christ. From the tiny group of supporters (or disciples) who gathered around him during his lifetime, it developed rapidly after his death and resurrection. Initially Jesus' followers operated as a group within Judaism, based in Jerusalem, and preached about their crucified leader as the Jewish Messiah who rose from the dead and was the Son of God. However, under the influence of Saint Paul, who had not been among Jesus' circle, the message was widened to appeal to Jews and non-Jews (Gentiles) alike. Paul is known as the 'Apostle to the Gentiles' and his three missionary journeys, around the eastern Mediterranean and Middle East, prefaced the spread of Christianity as a distinctive Church throughout the Roman Empire.

> 'Paul is the intellectual forebear of anyone who was brought up in the framework of once Christian Europe. He is one of a handful of towering figures who formed our way of thinking, and when you read his letters you are going back to your roots. You may not always like what you find, but you cannot get away from the fact that you have inherited his intellectual genes.'
> Broadcaster Edward Stourton in his 2004 book, *In the Footsteps of Saint Paul*

For its first millennium, the Catholic Church was the only institution in the Christian world, though in that period there were many practical and doctrinal disputes among its leaders as to how best to follow Jesus. Thereafter, successive splits, schisms and divisions, with Orthodox Christians in the East, and then with Lutherans, Protestants, Anglicans and many others in the West, left Christianity divided. Catholicism, however, remains Christianity's largest single organization and arguably its most influential.

An historical overview

The origins of Catholicism – and in particular of the role of the papacy at the head of the Church – are complex and will be examined in greater detail in subsequent chapters. However, in considering a Church that has defied all predictions of its demise and has endured for 2,000 years, it is important at the outset to give a brief historical overview.

Saint Peter, Jesus' chosen leader for his fledgling Church, worked after Christ's death with the other Apostles, and especially with Saint Paul, a Greek-speaking convert who joined them, to carry the new faith beyond Jerusalem and Judaism. In AD 64 both Peter and Paul were executed on the orders of the Roman Emperor, Nero. It is said that Peter was crucified upside down and that his body was buried on the spot in Rome where today stands the mother church of world Catholicism, the Basilica of St Peter's. In 1950 Pope Pius XII announced to the world that archaeologists had found evidence of Peter's tomb underneath the basilica.

Key idea

The supreme authority of the papacy in Catholicism, and therefore of the current incumbent, Pope Francis, rests on him being in a direct line all the way back to Saint Peter. Jesus himself chose Peter as the leader of his Church.

It was only in the late second century, however, that Peter began to be described as the first Bishop of Rome and as Pope (from *papa*, the Latin for 'father'). As the fledgling Church grew in size, despite fierce persecution from the Roman authorities, it started to imitate the hierarchical leadership model of the Roman Empire. Hence the development of the office of the Pope at the head of the Catholic Church and the role given to bishops as leaders of local communities of Christians. Eventually, in 312, the Emperor Constantine attached Christianity's emblem to the banner of his troops and it became the official religion of the empire.

When the western part of that empire slowly crumbled in the fourth and fifth centuries, the papacy managed to retain its power and influence in the chaos that ensued. Under exceptional leaders like Pope Gregory the Great (590–604; in this book all dates given for popes will signify their periods in office), it successfully evangelized the pagan forces that were destroying the Roman Empire and so laid the basis for a whole new Christian civilization in the West.

In the eleventh century there was a break with Christians in the East – the Orthodox – and this has never subsequently been mended. With the Renaissance of the fourteenth and fifteenth centuries, the dominance of papal, Catholic Christendom across Europe was undermined by social, economic and cultural factors. A German monk, Martin Luther, at the start of the sixteenth century, dealt a heavy blow to the authority of the Pope, setting up his own Church. His lead was followed by other Protestant reformers, but at the Council of Trent (1545–63) Catholicism regrouped as an instinctively traditional force for much of the next four centuries.

The advent of Pope John XXIII (1958–63) unleashed a period of what he called *aggiornamento*, or 'opening a window on the world'. The Church's hostility to anything perceived as 'new' was ended and Catholicism was renewed and reinvigorated at the landmark Second Vatican Council (1962–5). Old prejudices against other Christian Churches were replaced by a commitment to mutual exploration of common ground. Constructive engagement with the outside world blossomed, with a high premium placed on social justice rather than older notions of charitable work.

Key idea

Though the Catholic Church often presents itself as an unchanging institution, resistant to trends of the moment, it has in fact over the course of 2,000 years changed many times. In its capacity for adaptation is found its ability to survive and flourish.

This commitment to be part of the modern world found eloquent expression in the high-profile involvement of John Paul II (1978–2005) in the struggle to end Soviet communism's grip on his native Poland and Eastern Europe, which culminated in the fall of the Berlin Wall in 1989. And his successor but one, the Argentinian Pope Francis (2013–), has continued that trend, with his popularity on the world stage.

Spotlight

Many Catholics remark on the parallels between the reforming Pope John XXIII and Pope Francis – both new brooms in the Vatican, both intent on introducing wide-scale reform, and both having a personal charisma that is equally attractive to Catholics and non-Catholics.

How are Catholics different from other Christians?

Other members of the wider Christian family share the same model in the life, teachings, death and resurrection of Jesus Christ, but the Catholic Church is unique in its claim that its head, the Pope, stands in a direct line back to Saint Peter.

Peter, a married fisherman on the Sea of Galilee, was originally known as Simon. However, Jesus gave him a new name – *Kephas* in Aramaic, the language he would have spoken, meaning 'rock'. The Greek translation of this is rendered in English as Peter. 'You are Peter,' Jesus tells him in Chapter 16 of Saint Matthew's Gospel (one of four accounts in the New Testament of Jesus' life), 'and on this rock I will build my Church... I will give you the gates of the kingdom of heaven: whatever you bind on earth shall be considered bound in heaven.'

Spotlight

The gospels report that Saint Peter was married, as Jesus' touch cures Peter's mother-in-law from a fever. No mention is made of what happened to Peter's wife, but all popes since have not married.

The 'Apostolic Succession' – the idea that Jesus' mandate to Peter has been passed on to each and every one of his 265 successors as Pope – lies at the very core of Catholicism. The Pope has supreme authority within the Church for interpreting Christ's teachings. This has been its custom from earliest times, but was given formal recognition in 1870 when it was declared that the Pope can, when he wishes, speak infallibly on matters of faith and morals. He cannot make mistakes, Catholicism teaches, because he is being guided by the Holy Spirit. Like other Christian faiths, Catholicism is Trinitarian, that is, it believes that there are three persons in the One God: God, the Father, Jesus, his son, and the Holy Spirit.

But it is not only the paramount role of the Pope that marks out Catholicism. The Church's practice of the faith, especially its rigorous emphasis on the duty to attend the sacraments regularly and on questions of personal and public morality, also distinguishes it from other Christian churches.

Catholicism prides itself, too, on standing apart from trends in broader society and defending what it describes as 'eternal truths'. It is said that its attitudes move not in months, years or even decades, but over the course of centuries. It says of itself that it has never compromised teachings handed down by Jesus Christ to the Apostles because it does not have the authority to override scripture. Therefore it cannot, for example, ordain women to its priesthood because Jesus did not choose women among his 12 original Apostles.

The claim never to change its stance on such 'God-made' teachings is, however, disputed. Catholic interpretation of some key passages in the four gospels has certainly altered over the centuries, as will be discussed in subsequent chapters. What is undeniably true, though, is that Catholicism has often found itself at odds with the mores and morality of the society in which it has operated from Renaissance times onwards. In recent times, for example, Pope John Paul II (1978–2005) was fond of remarking that Catholicism was 'a sign of contradiction' in an increasingly secular modern society.

Though many outside the Catholic Church use the term 'Roman Catholics' to describe those who accept the *magisterium* – or supreme teaching authority – of the popes, based in the Vatican in Rome, many of those inside the Church refer to themselves simply as Catholics. This can occasionally lead to confusion. There are, for instance, those within Anglicanism who call themselves Catholic, imitating many features of Roman liturgy, but rejecting the supreme authority of the Pope.

Spotlight

The seventeenth-century Puritan poet John Milton dismissed the phrase 'Roman Catholic': 'And whereas the papist boasts himself to be a Roman Catholic, it is a mere contradiction, one of the pope's bulls [or official letters], as if he should say universal particular; a Catholic schismatic.' The exact origin of the term is not known, but it is unlikely to have been the papacy.

The distinguishing features of Catholicism

▶ **Its history:** Catholicism's survival and continuing success in attracting additional members globally after 2,000 years give it a certain identity and self-confidence. Some Church theologians see an organic growth over those two millennia, picturing Catholicism as a gigantic old tree, in a state of permanent development, shedding dead branches and poor fruit, as it matures towards an ultimate perfection.

▶ **The role of the papacy:** Though it was not until 1870 that the Pope was declared infallible 'in matters of faith and morals', in practice the authority of the papacy has given a unique definition to Catholic teaching throughout the ages.

▶ **Its priesthood:** The Catholic priesthood remains reserved, in all but a tiny handful of cases, to celibate men. The Church twins vocation to the priesthood with vocation to celibacy. Women remain excluded from the priesthood on the grounds of their gender.

▶ **Its teachings:** The Catholic Church goes against current secular norms by teaching that divorce, masturbation, sex before and outside marriage, homosexual relationships and all artificial means of contraception are sinful. It will not sanction the use by its faithful of condoms, even if their intention is to block the spread of HIV/AIDS, on the grounds that they would prevent the transmission of life. Pro-life in the widest sense, Catholicism opposes not only abortion but also the death penalty, while it promotes access to better education, health care, employment and housing for the needy of the world.

▶ **Its liturgy:** While Latin is no longer the standard language of the Catholic liturgy (its church services) around the globe, the Church continues to stand apart from other Christian faiths in its insistence, as part of its belief in what is called transubstantiation, that at the moment of consecration, during the celebration of the Eucharist (Holy Communion), Christ is present in the bread and wine in more than a symbolic way.

▶ **Its practices:** The Catholic Church requires weekly attendance of Mass; encourages veneration of Jesus' mother, the Blessed Virgin Mary, and 'the company of saints'; strongly encourages prayers for the dead as a way of interceding on their behalf to speed their journey; and endorses claims of miraculous cures achieved either through the intercession of those individuals it has chosen posthumously to declare saints, or by attendance at one of a number of officially sanctioned shrines. While no one of these practices is unique to Catholicism, together they form a body of behaviour that distinguishes the Catholic Church from other Churches and can, on occasion, cause controversy.

▶ **The emphasis it places on the role of the Holy Spirit:** Catholicism, like other Christian Churches, teaches of the Trinity, the three persons in One God, but it gives the Spirit certain distinctive roles: in enabling communication with Christ, in bestowing 'gifts of the Spirit' on believers, in promoting the unity of the Church and, even, in guiding the cardinal electors when they choose a new pope.

Attitudes to other faiths

Once Christianity had expanded beyond its original Jewish
base, it sought to play down its Jewish roots in order to form
its own distinctive identity. This led to its being responsible,
for many centuries, for encouraging the scapegoating of
Jews, accusing them of deicide – killing the Son of God. In
the aftermath of the Protestant Reformation of the sixteenth
century, Catholicism also came to regard newer Christian
Churches with great hostility.

However, these prejudices were definitively rejected at the
Second Vatican Council. In the decades that have followed it,
the Catholic Church has expended a great deal of energy on
building better relationships with other faiths. One spectacular
high point was the gathering Pope John Paul II hosted in the
Italian city of Assisi in October 1986, when he stood in a circle
with Anglicans, Buddhists, Hindus, Sikhs, Shintoists and African
and Amerindian animists who passed around a pipe of peace.
The event, John Paul said, 'has taught us anew to be aware of
the common origin and the common destiny of humanity'.

Particular emphasis has been given to entering into dialogues
with other mainstream Protestant Churches. This led, in the
1970s and 1980s, to hopes of an eventual Christian reunion.
Much common ground was eventually found.

Case study: Agreement on justification

In 1999 the Catholic Church and the Lutheran World Federation,
acting as the successors of Martin Luther, issued a Joint
Declaration to announce that they had reached agreement on one
of the key issues that had divided them since the Reformation –
that of justification.

Luther insistence that, through Jesus' sacrifice of himself on the cross of Calvary, each individual's sins were redeemed caused his final break with Catholicism, as well as the many wars that followed in the name of religion. In Luther's view, because of Jesus' death, the sinner is saved – or 'justified' – by his or her faith alone. The Catholic Church, though, staunchly rejected this view, and instead emphasized the need for believers to do 'good works' carried out over a lifetime so as to get a place in heaven. And these good works included donations made to the St Peter's rebuilding fund – another flash point between the two sides.

Almost 500 years later, the Joint Declaration showed how much the Catholic Church had changed in its attitudes to other Churches. Here it was prepared to lay to rest the longest-standing disagreement between it and Lutherans. The two Churches had come, they said, to a 'common understanding' on the question. It was quite a milestone.

And the same spirit was invoked again when the Vatican and the Lutheran World Federation announced plans a joint celebration of the 500th anniversary of the Reformation in 2017. 'The reasons for mutually condemning each other's faith', they said, 'have fallen by the wayside.' So the man who broke Catholicism's stranglehold on Christianity across Europe is, five centuries later, to be celebrated by the Pope himself.

However, other discussions between the different Christian Churches have stalled over key doctrinal questions such as Eucharist, ministry and the papacy, where Catholic teaching and practice are at odds with what occurs in its 'sister' organizations. In spite of these remaining theological obstacles, though, there is now much goodwill and practical co-operation, especially at grass-roots level, as seen, for example, in Catholic participation in annual Weeks of Prayer for Christian Unity and in national pan-Christian Councils of Churches.

With other non-Christian faiths, there have also been great steps forward. The 1965 Second Vatican Council document *Nostra Aetate* repudiated the idea that Jews had been responsible for deicide when Jesus was crucified. 'The death of Christ is not to be attributed to an entire people then alive,' it states, 'and even less to a people today. Therefore, let priests be careful not to say anything, in catechetical instruction or in preaching, that might give rise to hatred or contempt of the Jews in the hearts of their hearers.' All forms of anti-Semitism were repudiated. In the case of Islam, successive popes have worked to develop a relationship with Muslim leaders founded on mutual respect and tolerance of the practice of each other's faith.

Key idea

Though its history has often been one of hostility to other religions, modern Catholicism works closely with other faiths on both practical and theological issues, and teaches its followers to respect the religious beliefs of others outside the Catholic Church.

Nonetheless, at its core, Catholicism teaches that the 'Church of Christ' subsists within the Catholic Church. Therefore, it, rather than other faiths, represents the best route to salvation and eternal life with God. The Church has never abandoned its demand that its faithful evangelize those they meet.

The tension between these core beliefs and Catholic efforts to promote inter-faith dialogue was highlighted in July 2007, when the Vatican's Congregation for the Doctrine of the Faith published a document setting out with uncomfortable clarity that other Christian denominations 'cannot be called Churches in the proper sense'. Eastern Orthodoxy, perhaps the closest cousin to Catholicism in the wider Christian family, was labelled as 'wounded' because it does not accept the supreme authority of the Pope.

Key idea

Much has been accomplished to narrow the gap between Catholicism and other faiths, but it continues to believe it represents the best way – if not the only way – to God.

Conclusion

Though the modern Catholic Church sees itself as part of a wider Christian family, and maintains good relationships with other Churches and faiths at international, national and local level, it also retains a distinct and unchanging identity. This is based on its particular interpretations of the gospels, its own traditions and practices and – most obviously – on its loyalty to the Pope and the *magisterium* (teaching authority) of the Church. Both as a focus of unity in a global Church, and as a final decision-maker on disputed questions of faith and morals, the papacy enjoys great power, while the activities and pronouncements of individual popes, on the world stage, inevitably serve to draw attention to Catholicism, often at the expense of the more collective leaderships of other faiths.

Dig deeper

Thomas Bokenkotter, *A Concise History of the Catholic Church* (Doubleday, 1990).

Hans Kung, *The Catholic Church: A Short History* (Weidenfeld & Nicolson, 2001).

Father Alban McCoy, *An Intelligent Person's Guide to Catholicism* (Continuum, 2008).

Peter Stanford (ed.), *Why I am Still a Catholic* (Continuum, 2005).

Fact-check

1 How many Catholics are there in the world now?
   a   1.229 million
   b   12.29 million
   c   1.229 billion
   d   12.29 billion

2 Which country has the largest Catholic population?
   a   Mexico
   b   USA
   c   Philippines
   d   Brazil

3 Which country, as a percentage of its population, has the highest proportion of Catholics?
   a   Malta
   b   The Vatican
   c   Ireland
   d   Italy

4 Who was in the forefront in taking the Christian message to a non-Jewish audience?
   a   Peter
   b   Matthew
   c   Judas
   d   Paul

5 When or by whom was the Bishop of Rome first referred to as the Pope?
   a   In the gospels
   b   During the Reformation
   c   In the late second century
   d   By Jesus

6 What is the apostolic succession?
   a   A ladder that leads to heaven
   b   The link between Peter and all subsequent popes
   c   A box passed from pope to pope
   d   A ring that popes wear

7 Over what matters is the Pope infallible?
   a Of faith and morals
   b Of sexual ethics
   c Everything
   d Of the justification for war

8 Which word best sums up Catholicism's relationship with other faiths today?
   a friendly
   b hostile
   c competitive
   d dismissive

9 How does Catholicism regard Martin Luther today?
   a As a heretic
   b As a saint
   c As irrelevant
   d As someone it broadly agrees with

10 Which language will you hear wherever you attend a Catholic Mass?
   a English
   b Latin
   c the local one
   d Italian

Once a Catholic

In this chapter you will learn:

▶ *how attitudes have changed recently within Catholicism*
▶ *about the importance of tradition*
▶ *about the place of Mary.*

The changing Church

Notions of what it means to be a Catholic have shifted radically within the last 50 years as both society and the Church have changed. Within the Church, there used to be a popular argument, when confronted with internal dissent, that being a Catholic was akin to joining a club. If you didn't agree with its rules, you should leave, rather than demand change or flout the laws. An element of that fierce loyalty still exists, but today priests and bishops accept – privately and sometimes publicly – that they can no longer command their congregations as once they did. There is a more thoughtful attitude to faith and practice, still guided by a profound respect for the teaching authority of the Pope and his bishops, but no longer the sort of unquestioning obedience once associated with Catholics. The Church has returned to its original understanding of the word 'obedience' – namely to hear and therefore to understand and assent unless conscience dictates otherwise.

> *'If I am obliged to bring religion into after-dinner toasts, I shall drink to the Pope, if you please, – still to Conscience first, and to the Pope afterwards.'*
>
> Blessed John Henry Newman (1801–90), convert English cardinal, in a letter of 1874

Outside the Church, once-popular stereotypes of Catholics have fallen by the wayside as the world has come to recognize the diversity of belief among Catholics. It used to be expected, for example, that Catholics would usually be members of large families because of their Church's prohibition on the use of artificial contraceptives. Yet today, in many of the parishes of the developed world countries, most families will have, at most, two or three children.

Spotlight

When questioned about the ideal size of a Catholic family, when travelling back in January 2015 from a visit to the Philippines, Pope Francis remarked that it was not a requirement of Catholicism to breed 'like rabbits' and counselled that three children was in his opinion about the right number.

Likewise, Catholics have a reputation for being riven by guilt, especially over sex. Again in the popular mind, this is an attitude that has been instilled in impressionable young Catholics by their teachers, especially nuns. However, it is an out-dated image. The number of nuns teaching in schools has fallen dramatically, while approaches to sex and sexuality in Catholicism are becoming more nuanced and more accepting of the reality of people's lives. Marriage remains an ideal, for instance, but is no longer seen simply as the correct forum for sexual activity but rather as a covenant of life and love between two heterosexual adults.

Guilt is no more prevalent in a new generation of Catholics than in the wider world. Whether the stereotype was ever true is a matter of dispute, though the novels of Catholic writers such as Graham Greene, Evelyn Waugh, Edna O'Brien and David Lodge present a strong case for the proposition.

> 'Living in sin, with sin, by sin, for sin, every hour, every day, year in, year out. Waking up with sin in the morning, seeing the curtains drawn on sin, bathing it, dressing it, clipping diamonds to it, feeding it, showing it round, giving it a good time, putting it to sleep at night with a tablet of Dial if it's fretful. Always the same, like an idiot child carefully nursed, guarded from the world.'
> Julia Flyte, reflecting on Catholic guilt in Evelyn Waugh's
> *Brideshead Revisited* (1945)

Was Jesus Catholic?

No, he was a Jew and the origins of Christianity are as a reform movement within Judaism. The Catholic Church believes that Jesus' mission was not only for Jews but for the whole world. His intention was therefore, according to Catholic teaching, to found a new Church, close to but distinct from Judaism. This wish was carried through after Jesus' death when his message was taken to non-Jews or Gentiles.

The Catholic Church shares with other Christian Churches the aspiration to model itself on Jesus. 'He is "the perfect man", who invites us to become his disciples and follow him,' states the 1993 official rulebook, *Catechism of the Catholic Church*. 'In humbling himself, he has given us an example to imitate, through his prayer he draws us to pray, and by his poverty he calls on us to accept freely the privation and persecutions that may come our way.' Other Christian Churches have a similar approach.

Catholicism, moreover, teaches that it is Jesus, not the Pope, who is actually head of the Church and that he continues to dwell on earth in the form of the Catholic Church, until his return in the Second Coming. Again, this is not unique. One distinguishing factor in the Catholic position – compared with, for example, Evangelical or fundamentalist Christianity – is its view that salvation is not limited to those who attend the sacraments of the Catholic Church. Jesus is, Catholicism holds, 'the universal sacrament of salvation', and hence is available to all, whatever their creed and regardless of whether they are Catholics.

Spotlight

My own Catholic upbringing was traditional, and it was not until I was in my twenties that a friend took me to his synagogue for a service. As I looked round, I said, 'It looks very like a church.' My friend smiled. 'It's the other way round. Churches look very like synagogues.'

What do Catholics believe?

An older generation of Catholics will recall that they learned their faith not principally through reading the Bible, but instead through instruction from their priests and nuns, through their Catholic schools, and through the Catholic liturgy. The origin of this oral approach to conveying the essentials of Catholic beliefs lies in times when the vast majority of the population was illiterate and therefore unable to read scripture. However, it endured in Catholicism long after increasing levels of literacy had permitted other Christian denominations a greater concentration on individual study of the Bible as a way of learning how to be a true follower of Jesus Christ.

Catholicism, by contrast, continued into the twentieth century to see it as the role of the priest to pass on the beliefs and practice of the faith to his congregation. The priest acted as a kind of intermediary between God and his people. Because humankind was regarded as essentially sinful, there was an obligation assumed by the clergy to guide the faithful away from wrongful interpretation of key biblical ideas and from resulting sinful behaviour. Catholics were largely discouraged from individual biblical study and towards conformity with the traditional practices of their Church.

It was only in 1909 that Pope Pius X founded the Pontifical Biblical Institute in Rome to encourage critical study of the scriptures. So, in recent times, Catholicism has, in a real sense, returned to being a 'religion of the book', with a new emphasis placed on scriptural study by clergy and laity alike, albeit alongside the more usual standbys of papal pronouncements and official rulebooks such as the old *Penny Catechism* and its successor, the 1993 *Catechism of the Catholic Church*.

Key idea

Catholicism has long been fond of lists and formulae as an easy way for people to remember the principal teachings of their Church. The various versions of the *Catechism*, with their numbered entries covering every aspect of life and giving official guidance on how to approach it, are just one aspect of this taste for calibration.

The place of tradition and prayer

One time-honoured route in Catholicism to instilling an instinctive understanding of the faith was through what was called 'liturgical prayer'. The Church aimed to distil the essence of Catholicism into the words of the prayers that make up the liturgy or Mass. So, for example, through the Apostles' Creed, all necessary key doctrines were transmitted to and absorbed by the faithful as they constantly repeated the words. This was an approach known in Church circles by the Latin phrase *Lex orandi, lex credendi*, which translates as 'the law of prayer is the law of belief'. In other words, what you say out loud in the liturgy is what you believe.

This ancient Christian principle dates back to the early centuries of the Church, before there was an agreed canon of scriptural texts. It was only in the early fifth century that Saint Jerome produced his Vulgate, an officially sanctioned translation into Latin of those books of the Old and New Testament that the Catholic Church was willing to sanction as its Bible. Many previously revered texts were excluded. They are known today as the 'Apocrypha', from the Greek word for things that have been 'hidden away', and can tell a very different story of Jesus from the Authorized Version.

The 'liturgical prayer' approach was used throughout the Church's history to allow its leaders to place, above the views of individual believers, an officially sanctioned interpretation of the extracts from scriptures included in the cycles of readings to be used in the Mass. The result of this process of transmission is what is sometimes called the *depositum fidei* – 'the deposit of the faith' – a phrase that embraces both the Bible and the interpretation of it made through the *magisterium* of the Church down through the ages.

Catholicism places a greater emphasis than other Christian denominations on the force of its own traditions. If the Church has always regarded something as morally unacceptable, Catholicism's firm presumption will be that shifting attitudes in outside society are no reason to change its own mind.

Key idea

The tradition of the Church is as important in shaping Catholic teaching and attitudes as the scriptures and sayings of Jesus.

But, as Pius X acknowledged in 1909, such a system was open to abuse and risked treating the scriptures as if they were straightforward, black-and-white documents. They are not, and they contain many passages, open to a variety of interpretations, which demand to be read in the context of their times. In the case of the New Testament, for example, passages may have been added to the original oral accounts of Jesus' life in order to depict him as fulfilling Old Testament prophecies.

Equally, the four gospels, the official version of Jesus' time on earth, were written between 30 and 100 years after his death by scribes who may not have been eyewitnesses to the events they purport to describe. They are also, in places, contradictory. Only two of the gospels, for instance, include an account of Jesus' birth in Bethlehem, and only Luke's gospel presents the traditional picture of the manger and stable.

Key idea

Catholics today are encouraged and supported by the Church to study, reflect on and explore the gospels for themselves.

It becomes yet more complicated because Jesus did not speak in the gospels specifically on many of the moral dilemmas that confront contemporary Christianity and over which Catholicism takes such a firm stand. For example, he makes no reference at all to homosexuality, though it undoubtedly existed at that time. So Catholicism has based its centuries-old teaching that homosexuality is 'a strong tendency towards an intrinsic moral evil', as the Vatican reiterated in a 1986 document, on a reading of the general tone of Jesus' remarks on sexual morality, as well as earlier precedents in the Old Testament, along with its own stated position down the ages. It can be difficult for Catholics to distinguish between what are sometimes called 'God-made' (i.e. scriptural) and 'man-made' (i.e. dictated by the traditional practice of the Church) teachings.

Spotlight

You might see the decision of Saint Jerome and the Church Fathers to include not one gospel but four (and four different and sometimes contradictory accounts of Jesus' life at that) as an acknowledgement that there is more than one way to follow Jesus' example.

The role of Mary

The overlapping of tradition and scripture in Catholic belief and practice can be seen in the unique stress the Church places on Mary, the mother of Jesus. Catholicism holds that Mary plays a special role in humankind's salvation, intervening on our behalf with her son.

Some Catholics would rate her even more highly. In 1997, 4.35 million signatures were collected for an appeal to declare her 'Co-Redemptrix, Mediatrix of All Graces and Advocate for the People'. Pope John Paul II rejected the notion, on the advice of a Vatican commission, but throughout his pontificate promoted Mary as the supreme example of a Catholic woman and of how women should live their lives. He even placed the letter M at a central point in his papal coat of arms.

> *'Whether we regard the Virgin Mary as the most sublime and beautiful image in man's struggle towards the good and the pure, or the most pitiable production of ignorance and superstition, she represents a central theme in the history of Western attitudes to women. She is one of the few female figures to have attained the status of a myth.'*
>
> Convent-educated historian Marina Warner in
> *Mary: Alone of All Her Sex* (1976)

Yet she features briefly in the gospels' accounts and little of what has later been claimed for her by Catholicism has any basis in the Bible. This is something the Church freely acknowledges. 'What the Catholic faith believes about Mary is based on what it believes about Christ,' the *Catechism* of the Catholic Church states plainly.

Key idea

Mary, Jesus' mother, plays a special role in Catholicism that is based more on its traditions than on her prominence in the gospel accounts.

As the Church believes that Jesus was at once both human and divine – son of God and a man – it follows that his mother must have been an exceptional human being. So in Matthew's and Luke's gospels – but not in Mark's or John's – it is told that Mary gave birth to Jesus without first having sexual intercourse. Jesus' birth was a virgin birth. Traditional Catholicism used to describe the actual delivery as 'like light passing through glass'.

If the Virgin Birth divides the gospel writers, Catholic teaching about the Immaculate Conception – the belief that Mary, unlike the rest of humankind, was born without the stain of original sin which was, for everyone else, a shared legacy since Adam and Eve's fall in the Garden of Eden – receives only an oblique endorsement from Luke. He describes how the Angel Gabriel, on coming down from heaven to tell Mary that she is to bear God's son (known in Christianity as the Annunciation), greets her as 'full of grace'. From this phrase, Church Fathers down the ages have developed the notion that Mary was, as the *Universal Catechism* puts it, 'wholly borne by God's grace'. It continues: 'Through the centuries the Church has become ever more aware that Mary, "full of grace" through God, was redeemed from the moment of her conception.' The doctrine – or official teaching – of the Immaculate Conception dates back to 1854.

Key idea

Catholicism teaches that Mary gave birth to Jesus without first having sex – the Virgin Birth. It also teaches that she was born without the stain of original sin – the Immaculate Conception. The two are often mixed up.

There is no scriptural basis at all for the third principal claim that Catholicism makes on Mary's behalf – its teaching that she was assumed body and soul into heaven when her earthly life ended. For all others, Catholicism teaches that the body is discarded and only the soul endures. However, Mary was set apart from this in 1950 by Pope Pius XII, who in doing so exercised the power, acquired in 1870, for popes to speak infallibly in matters of faith and morals.

Though the idea of Mary's Assumption, body and soul, into heaven was unknown in the early Church, she has been exalted by leading theologians throughout Church history. Saint Irenæus, bishop of Lyons in France in the second century, for example, is sometimes called the first theologian 'of the Virgin Mother'. He made a parallel, still repeated in Catholicism to this day, between Eve and Mary, urging that,

> as the former was led astray by an angel's discourse to fly from God after transgressing his word, so the latter by an angel's discourse had the gospel preached unto her that she might bear God, obeying his word. And if the former had disobeyed God, yet the other was persuaded to obey God: that the Virgin Mary might become an advocate for the virgin Eve. And as mankind was bound unto death through a virgin, it is saved through a virgin; by the obedience of a virgin the disobedience of a virgin is compensated.

How such polarized attitudes to Mary and Eve within Catholicism have shaped its attitudes to the role of women is a matter for later chapters. What is important to note here is that, although official declarations of doctrine concerning the Virgin Mary are of relatively recent provenance, devotion to her has been a distinctive feature of Catholicism throughout its history. There is, for example, the tradition of reported apparitions of the Virgin Mary on earth, in her role as an intermediary between God and his people. In 352 a Roman nobleman, John, and his childless wife were convinced that the Virgin Mary came to them and miraculously intervened on their behalf to allow them to become parents. The Virgin's sign had been a snowflake falling on one of the Seven Hills of Rome and so a church was built in memory of Our Lady of the Snows where today stands the basilica of St Mary Major.

In 1061 a Saxon noblewoman, Richeldis de Faverches, reported that Mary transported her from Walsingham, Norfolk, in the east of England, back to her own home in Nazareth. As a result, Lady Richeldis subsequently built a shrine to the Virgin in Walsingham, which became a major centre of pilgrimage, attracting kings, queens and scholars, until Henry VIII ordered its dissolution in 1537 during the English Reformation.

Spotlight

The medieval shrine at Walsingham featured a 'Holy House', a replica of Jesus' childhood home in Nazareth. Some traders in the town took this domestic image to extremes and would sell pilgrims bottles of white liquid, claiming it was Mary's breast milk. Their excesses caused the Dutch Catholic theologian and reformer Erasmus to rename the place, when he visited in the 1520s, as 'Falsingham'.

Popular world sites of Marian devotion

Lourdes, in south-western France, where, Catholics believe, Mary appeared 18 times in 1858 to a 14-year-old local girl, Bernadette Soubirous. The Virgin made a fountain spring up in a grotto at the site of the apparition and its water is believed to have miraculous healing powers. The shrine was inaugurated in 1873 and is among the best-known sites of pilgrimage in Catholic Europe.

Knock, in County Mayo, is Ireland's national shrine. In 1879 a silent Mary, along with her husband, Joseph, and John the Evangelist, is reported to have appeared to 15 local people. In 1979 Pope John Paul II visited Knock during his tour of Ireland.

Fatima, where, for six consecutive months in 1917, Mary is said to have appeared in a blinding light to three peasant children in Portugal. Others at the scene saw the sun dance. Mary urged the seers to do penance, say the Rosary and pray for the conversion of Russia from communism. She also imparted three secrets. The first two – a vision of hell and guidance on how to save souls in hell – were made public, but it was only in 2000 that the Vatican revealed the third secret, a vision of a Pope-like figure being struck down by assailants, taken to be a reference to the 1981 assassination attempt in St Peter's Square by a lone Turkish gunman on John Paul II who was a particular devotee of Our Lady of Fatima.

Częstochowa, in southern Poland, is home to the Jasna Góra Monastery, which houses the Black Madonna. Catholic legend states that this painting of Mary was done by Luke, the gospel writer, on a tabletop from the home of Jesus and his parents. It was brought to Częstochowa in 1382 from Jerusalem and is reported to have saved the Poles from foreign invaders.

Garabandal, in north-west Spain, was visited by the Virgin Mary many times between 1961 and 1965, according to four young girls. She gave them messages that urged the world to purify its heart and forgive sins. Though many pilgrims travel to the small village, the Catholic Church has officially discounted the visions.

Medjugorje, in Hercegovina, has, since June 1981, witnessed apparitions of the Virgin Mary – the 'Gospa' in the local Croatian language – to six seers, originally children, now adults. Her message of daily prayer and Bible reading, fasting and attendance of the sacraments has attracted many, but the Vatican has yet to give the shrine official sanction.

Key idea

Catholicism regards Mary as surpassing all others as a bridge between believers and God, and therefore endorses reports of her appearances at various shrines around the globe.

How Catholicism operates

The reforming Second Vatican Council declared that there should no longer be a division in Catholicism between those who are ordained and those who are not. Henceforth, it promised, both clergy and laity would be equal partners as 'the people of God'. That equality was rooted in a 'shared priesthood' of all Catholics, received at Baptism, but lived out in many different ways. The phrase 'the people of God', one of the most potent in Catholicism, occurs in the key Council document, *Lumen Gentium*, approved in November 1964. (Church documents often have Latin titles. *Lumen Gentium* translates as 'The Light of Nations'.)

The second chapter of *Lumen Gentium* – designated as a 'Constitution for the Church' – is entitled 'People of God', but is followed by a section called 'The Church is Hierarchical', which explains the essential leadership role of the Pope, cardinals, archbishops, bishops and priests within the Catholic community. In practice, Catholicism remains, in its structures and mindset, a highly centralized, global organization: its believers are organized into parishes and these make up dioceses headed by bishops, who report to archbishops and then cardinals who in turn both elect popes and carry through the teaching of the men they have chosen to lead them.

Key idea

The Church, in Catholic teaching, is not just an institution, or a hierarchical structure, but in the words of the Second Vatican Council 'the people of God'.

The Catholic Church is emphatically not a democracy. While popes hold regular synods on key issues such as the family, evangelization and the place of women, they are under no binding obligation to act on the views they hear expressed by the clerical and lay representatives from around the world who attend. Different popes interpret their teaching authority in a variety of ways. Among key concepts at the Second Vatican Council was that of collegiality – that groups of local bishops in a particular country could decide how best to act on issues in accordance with the overall principles of their Church, without seeking formal approval from the Vatican.

This practice was, however, eroded during the papacy of John Paul II who believed that too much local autonomy would destroy the unity of the Church. So, for example, when in 1983 bishops in the United States wanted to publish a teaching document on nuclear weapons, the Vatican insisted on seeing the text first and making substantial amendments. Since his election in 2013, however, Pope Francis has indicated his wish to delegate more powers from the Vatican and the papacy down to groups of local bishops.

Catholicism as a way of life

Approaches to Catholic education – both of children and of adults – have altered considerably, with a greater emphasis now placed on the positive imperatives of Catholic teaching, especially with regard to love of neighbour and wider social responsibility. Talk of sinfulness, especially with regard to sex, or of the Devil and hell, is, by contrast, muted in comparison with what was heard in the classroom and from the pulpit 50 years ago. Much effort has been made to ensure that those who fall short of Catholic ideals in their personal life (for example, those who divorce or have children out of wedlock) do not feel excluded from or rejected by the Church. This can cause tensions, especially when the reality of the warm welcome offered by parish communities to those whose lives do not conform to Church teachings is set alongside doctrinal statements from Church leaders reiterating the ideals that lie behind those teachings.

Spotlight

Though the Devil was routinely castigated in sermons in the medieval Church, Catholic priests rarely even mention him today. Pope John Paul II, who wrote, preached and broadcast more than any pontiff in recent times, made only passing references to the Devil. In his one substantive remark, at an audience with pilgrims in summer 1986, he said that the Devil and his demons 'were created good by God but have become evil by their own will'.

There are many people today, especially in the Western world, who describe themselves as lapsed or cultural Catholics, brought up in the faith, still attached to it in some ill-defined way, but no longer regular Mass-goers. One of the distinctive features of Catholicism appears to be the way in which even those who reject some or all of the teachings they received in their Catholic childhood retain an emotional and spiritual link with the Church ever after.

> 'I wouldn't be a very spiritual man, right? I don't believe in God, right? Still Catholic. Because there's nothing you can do when you're Catholic. Once you've started Catholic, frankly, there's no real way to stop being Catholic.'
>
> Irish comedian and TV presenter Dara O'Briain during a 2005 performance

The Catholic way of life today is built around the parish, the home and, where they are available, Catholic schools. A key feature is the obligation to attend Mass on Sundays and on a small number of Holy Days of Obligation throughout the year.

Holy Days of Obligation

These are decided by local bishops, who can move their commemoration to the nearest Sunday, but often include:

▶ 6 January, the Feast of the Epiphany, marking the arrival of the three kings at Jesus' birthplace
▶ The Thursday of the sixth week after Easter, known as Ascension Thursday, when Jesus' ascent into heaven is recalled
▶ 29 June, the Feast of Saints Peter and Paul
▶ 15 August, the Assumption, when Jesus' mother was raised body and soul into heaven.
▶ 1 November, All Saints' Day.

Key idea

On certain designated days of the year, in addition to every Sunday, Catholics are expected by the Church to attend Mass.

The sacramental life

The place of the seven sacraments is crucial in giving a structure to the Catholic way of life:

1 **Baptism** – welcoming infants into the family of the Church – usually takes place within the first six months after birth.

2 **The first reception of the sacrament of reconciliation** – once known as confession or penance – comes when the child is aged between seven and nine and immediately precedes first Holy Communion.

3 **Holy Communion** – receiving the bread and wine of the Eucharist as the body and blood of Christ – is the most central of the sacraments and is often referred to as 'the Bread of Life'.

4 **Confirmation** – making an adult commitment to the faith, before a bishop – usually comes in the mid-teens.

5 **The sacrament of marriage** – the partnership of the couple and God as the basis for family life – remains a foundation stone of the Catholic approach, even though marriage has declined in popularity in Western secular society.

6 **Ordination** – or holy orders – takes place when a man becomes a priest, after completing an average of eight years of study.

7 **The sacrament of the anointing of the sick** – formerly known as the Last Rites or Extreme Unction ('final anointing') – is administered by a priest to those who may be approaching death.

Key idea

Catholicism teaches that there are seven sacraments. Some Christian Churches follow this model, but most reduce the list, placing greatest emphasis on Baptism and Eucharist.

Is there a specific Catholic morality?

The Catholic Church, like all other religious bodies, has a body of teachings, many of which touch on principles of individual and societal moral conduct. It places particular emphasis on two areas: the first concerning what might loosely be called social justice (a favourite phrase of Pope Francis is that Catholicism should be 'a poor church, for the poor'), and the second involving pro-life issues. With regard to social justice, Catholicism, often through local bishops or development agencies such as the worldwide Caritas Internationalis network, is prominent in tackling economic injustice, political oppression and the abuse of human rights.

> 'Are we able to communicate the face of a Church which is "home" to all? We sometimes speak of a Church that has its doors closed, but here we are contemplating much more than a Church with open doors, much more!... We need to bring Christ to others, through these joys and hopes; we need to pass through the clouds of indifference without losing our way; we need to descend into the darkest night without being overcome and disoriented; we need to listen to the dreams, without being seduced; we need to share their disappointments, without becoming despondent; to sympathize with those whose lives are falling apart, without losing our own strength and identity.'
>
> Pope Francis in July 2013 speaking to the Brazilian bishops

The Church's social teaching is often called Catholicism's 'best-kept secret' and is contained in celebrated papal documents such as *Rerum Novarum* ('Of New Things'), *Pacem in Terris* ('On Establishing Universal Peace') and *Populorum Progressio* ('On the Development of Peoples'). The first of these, released in 1891 by Pope Leo XIII, supported the foundation of trade unions, laid the basis for the Christian Democratic parties of Europe in the twentieth century and attacked the notion that 'the wealthy and the working men are intended by nature to live in mutual conflict'.

The second, published by Pope John XXIII in 1963, in the wake of the erection of the Berlin Wall and the Cuban Missile Crisis, which had caused fears for the future of humankind, was addressed not just to Catholics but 'to all men of goodwill'. It rejected the arms race, urged negotiation and set out, on the basis of Christian teaching, a universal human right to 'bodily integrity and to the means which are suitable for the proper development of life'.

The third was an urgent and ringing appeal from Pope Paul VI in 1967, and addressed itself to the consequences of global economic inequality. 'The world is sick. The poor nations remain poor while the rich ones become still richer. The very life of poor nations, civil peace in developing countries and world peace itself are at stake.'

Key idea

Catholicism has a well-developed and widely respected philosophy of social justice that promotes greater equality, advocates narrowing the gap between rich and poor, and holds to account prevailing capitalism and market-oriented practices around the globe.

With regard to pro-life issues, the Catholic Church has taken an outspoken stance against anything that it believes interferes with the transmission of human life. In *Humanae Vitae* ('Of Human Life') in 1968, Pope Paul VI reiterated traditional Catholic teaching. The sexual act, he wrote, must 'retain its intrinsic relationship to the procreation of human life'. So the use of condoms or the contraceptive pill remained unlawful for Catholics because they directly contradicted the 'moral order which was established by God'. Furthermore, the Pope prohibited the 'direct interruption of the generative process already begun'. Abortion, even for therapeutic reasons, remained absolutely forbidden, as was sterilization.

By refusing to modify traditional teaching in this area – despite widespread pressure from lay Catholics and the pleadings of influential Catholic leaders – Pope Paul VI ensured that these particular distinctive teachings of Catholicism remained among its best known. In reality, many individual Catholics decided that, in good conscience, they could overlook the Pope's demands in these intensely personal areas.

However, in the face of such dissent, successive popes have declined to retreat from Paul VI's restatement of traditional values. Some, like Pope John Paul II, have extended them into new areas of moral uncertainty – notably questions of in vitro fertilization and genetic manipulation, both of which Catholicism opposes and which we will explore at greater length in subsequent chapters.

Case study: Lay Catholic opinion on Church teaching

In a major break with traditional practice, in the autumn of 2013 Pope Francis instructed the Vatican bureaucracy to send out an online questionnaire for completion by lay Catholics as part of the preparations for the Extraordinary Synod (or meeting of bishops) that he had called to discuss Church teaching on the family in October 2014. The 35 questions posed were sometimes written in very academic language, but they asked Catholics what they believed on such issues as marriage and divorce, birth control and same-sex marriages. The Pope was opening the door to dissent from official teaching on these matters, which had long been reported, but which until that point had never been measured by the Church authorities.

In many countries the local bishops decided not to publish in full the details of the responses to the questionnaires, in case, they said, it pre-empted the discussions at the Extraordinary Synod. However, in Germany, Switzerland and Luxembourg – together home to 28 million Catholics – the bishops did permit some of the findings to be made public. 'Most of the baptised have an image of the Church', said the German bishops, 'that, on the one hand, is family-friendly in attitude, but at the same time unrealistic in its attitude to sexual morality.' They reported that between 90 and 100 per cent of those who replied rejected Catholic teaching that sex should happen only once a couple has married. 'Many, in fact,' the bishops said, 'considered it irresponsible to marry without living together beforehand.'

And in Switzerland the bishops revealed that well over half of those who had filled in the questionnaire dissented from Catholic teaching that insists homosexuals should remain celibate and opposes same-sex unions. Sixty per cent of Swiss Catholic respondents were in favour of recognition of such unions and of Church blessing for them. The bishops did, however, also note that those Catholics in the minority on these particular questions held their negative opinions very strongly, raising the question whether, on such a topical and contemporary question, there is indeed any such thing as a single Catholic position.

Conclusion

Catholicism, arguably alone of world religions, continues to suffer criticism for holding attitudes – especially in relation to sexual morality – that have long since been modified by secular society. One of the reasons for this is that so much of Catholic teaching is based on tradition – both in moral questions and in practices – which in its turn was dictated by the particular circumstances of particular eras. It seems to bear little resemblance to the beliefs and practices of individual Catholics today. It is only by reading and studying the gospels, some Catholics argue, that a true picture of the correct behaviour for followers of Jesus in the modern world can be discerned.

Dig deeper

Eamon Duffy, *Saints and Sinners: A History of the Popes* (Yale, 1997).

Gerard Noel, *Anatomy of the Catholic Church* (Michael Russell, 1994).

Desmond Seward, *The Dancing Sun: Journeys to the Miracle Shrines* (Fount, 1993).

1 How many children did Pope Francis counsel Catholic families to have?
   a 1
   b 3
   c 6
   d 10

2 Who, according to Catholicism, is the real head of the Church?
   a Jesus
   b The Pope
   c The bishops
   d The 'people of God'

3 Which is the only gospel to tell of Jesus' birth in a stable in Bethlehem in a manger?
   a Matthew
   b Mark
   c Luke
   d John

4 According to Catholicism, which of the following best describes Jesus?
   a Human
   b Divine
   c Human and divine
   d None of the above?

5 Mary gave birth to Jesus without first having sex. How is this known in Catholicism?
   a The Immaculate Conception
   b The first miracle
   c Mary's gift
   d The Virgin Birth

6 What does the doctrine of the Assumption teach about what happened to Mary after her death?
   a That she was buried
   b That she was declared a saint
   c That she went up to heaven body and soul
   d That she appeared to the Apostles

7 Which of the following has *not* been a place where Mary is reported to have appeared?

 a Lourdes
 b Jerusalem
 c Fatima
 d Walsingham

8 What is Catholic family life traditionally built around?

 a Home, parish and school
 b Home and parish
 c Parish
 d Home

9 What event is celebrated on the 15 August in the Catholic calendar?

 a The Epiphany
 b The Feast of Peter and Paul
 c The Assumption
 d Easter Sunday

10 Which of the seven sacraments usually follows Holy Communion in Catholicism?

 a Reconciliation
 b Confirmation
 c Marriage
 d Ordination

Part Two

The history of Catholicism

The early Church

In this chapter you will learn:

▶ *why Catholicism made its base in Rome*
▶ *how it grew into a Church*
▶ *how it became a political power.*

There is, at first glance, an irony in the fact that Catholicism should be associated with Rome at all. Jesus lived and died in Palestine. How did a Middle Eastern religion end up with its global headquarters in Rome, especially as the Roman overlords of Jerusalem, in the shape of Pontius Pilate, were heavily involved in Jesus' execution?

The birth of the Catholic Church

In the immediate aftermath of the crucifixion, Jesus' original followers concentrated their preaching in Jerusalem among fellow Jews. However, a one-time persecutor of Jesus' disciples, Saul of Tarsus, underwent an extraordinary conversion experience on the road to Damascus where he saw a vision of Jesus. As a consequence, Saul became Paul and believed that Jesus' life, death and resurrection held a message that related not just to Jewish law and the prophecies of the Hebrew scriptures (called the Old Testament by Christians), but to the whole human race. He therefore began to spread the word enthusiastically around the Roman Empire, of which he (unlike the 12 original Apostles) was a citizen.

'The fact that the Gentile world adopted Christianity is owing almost solely to one man: Paul of Tarsus. Without Paul, it is highly unlikely that Christianity would ever have broken away from Jerusalem.'

A.N. Wilson on Paul in *The Mind of the Apostle* (1997)

Paul was joined in this missionary endeavour by Peter, named by Jesus to lead his followers after his death. Antioch became the first centre of this outreach to the Gentiles – non-Jews – and it was here that the term 'Christian' began to be used. 'It was at Antioch', records the Acts of the Apostles (11:26) 'that the disciples were first called "Christians".'

In Jerusalem, such developments were regarded with concern by figures such as James, described in the New Testament as Jesus' brother (though, according to Catholic tradition, in reality his stepbrother, the son of Mary's husband, Joseph, who had been married before but whose first wife had died). James was the leader of Jesus' followers in the city, and believed that their future lay as a group within Judaism.

The tensions between these two approaches were only partially resolved by a compromise reached at a council held in Jerusalem around AD 49. The momentum was strongly with Paul and Peter as they and their followers carried their wider interpretation of the teachings of Jesus to countless cities in the Roman Empire. This growth beyond Jewish roots became ever more marked when the Temple in Jerusalem, spiritual home of Judaism, was destroyed by the Roman occupiers in AD 70. The forces that were to make Christianity a world religion rather than a Jewish sect were gathering pace.

Key idea

Christianity grew out of Judaism, but quickly separated from it, and for many centuries had a troubled relationship with its own Jewish roots.

Rome, as capital of the empire and a magnet for scholars, was the obvious place to base the new Church. However, it did not afford Jesus' followers a warm welcome. They preached against almost everything that the Roman Empire held dear – its morality, its religion, its celebration of war and its culture. The early Christians therefore quickly proved controversial, making converts but also suffering persecution and even death at the hands of those who regarded their teachings as wrong-headed and dangerous.

The early years of the Catholic Church were characterized by constant, extraordinary growth, which took place despite (and, some historians suggest, because of) violent opposition from the Roman authorities. Peter and Paul were just two among those martyred for their faith. One of the most remarkable features of the early centuries of the Church was its unshakeable faith in its own beliefs, something that enabled it to withstand such persecution. Tertullian (155–230), a noted early Church leader, claimed that in the blood of martyrs was found the seed of the new Church.

Spotlight

Intrigued by the Christians' secret gatherings, the Romans let their imaginations get the better of them. They accused the Christians of incest, cannibalism and even of worshipping a god who was a donkey, and thus demonized the early Church. Later, when it was in power, the Church similarly demonized its opponents using similar slurs.

Another noteworthy aspect was the foresight of leaders who, amid such outpourings of zeal and chaos, were able to lay the foundations of an enduring institution with shared beliefs and practices. It was a task that they undertook even though they were convinced that the Second Coming – the return in triumph of Jesus to earth – was imminent.

How the institution was created

There were three, often controversial, aspects to the work of the early Church Fathers, as the first leaders of Christianity are known, in fashioning a Church:

1 The creation of a class of elders who became, by the second century, deacons, priests and bishops, and who were eventually all male.

2 The collecting of an authoritative set of apostolic writings, and discarding of many other 'apocryphal' texts and gospels, a process that continued up to and including the fifth century, with Saint Jerome and his definitive Latin translation of the Bible, known as the Vulgate.

3 Reaching agreement on a set of basic beliefs by which Christians would live.

These three were not achieved quickly, or without rancour, or even simultaneously. By AD 160 the system of hierarchical government that remains to this day a distinguishing feature of the Catholic Church had all but been established. One vital factor in this was the belief that each leader, 'ordained' to his ministry by the laying on of hands by those already 'ordained', could therefore trace a line back to Peter and hence Jesus. Again, this is something that is still part of Catholic belief about its priesthood today.

Spotlight

The role of an elder in the early Church became a point of dispute during the Reformation. John Calvin, one of the leading Protestant dissenters against Rome, created the role of elder, a non-cleric who joined in both the democratic decision-making process of the Church and the provision of pastoral care. He was a priest/minister without being ordained. In the early Church, Calvin argued, there were lay elders who were the equal of clerical bishops. He quoted the Acts of the Apostles, the account of the early Church in the New Testament: 'In each of these churches, they appointed elders, and with prayer and fasting, they commanded them to the Lord in whom they had come to believe.'

It took some time for the role of the Pope – and his supreme authority over the Church – to be firmly established in practice, though it was endorsed in theory. It was only in the middle years of the fifth century, during the papacy of Leo the Great (one of very few popes to be accorded that title by Catholicism), that one can truly say the writ of the Bishop of Rome prevailed to any wide extent.

Agreement on a 'canon' of accepted writings also took several centuries. There were groups who took different views in the early centuries. The Gnostics, for example, derived from scripture an essentially pessimistic and 'dualistic' view of life on earth, seeing the 'good' soul as trapped on earth in 'evil' human flesh. They therefore hankered after death and afterlife. They were condemned as heretics and exiled from the new Church. Then there were those in the second century, for example, who felt that Saint John's gospel, so different in tone and approach from the other three in the New Testament, should be excluded. Other 'gospels', ascribed among others to the Apostle Thomas – this basic account of Jesus' key sayings is thought to be the earliest written record of his life, produced within ten years of his death – were excluded, along with more impressionistic versions attributed to Judas Iscariot, Mary Magdalene and Philip. Consensus was not reached on such matters until towards the end of the fourth century.

Key idea

While the four gospel accounts of Jesus' life cannot be taken literally as eyewitness accounts, they should be taken seriously as historical documents, especially when compared with some of the other chronologically later texts that also claim to be gospels.

The establishment of the rules by which Christians should live greatly preoccupied the early Church Fathers such as Irenæus of Lyons (130–202), whose writings were widely circulated, as well as the regular 'synods' or meetings of bishops from all the centres of Christianity. It was the Council of Nicaea (325) that finally agreed a creed or statement of key beliefs, known ever after as the Nicene Creed.

The word 'catholic', meaning universal, was used very early on in Christianity's history to denote its ambitions to be the religion of all. A letter written by Saint Ignatius of Antioch (d.107) to Christians in the Greek city of Smyrna just before his death, for example, contains the term 'Catholic Church'. By this, Ignatius was describing Christianity in its universal sense, but excluding heretics, such as those rejecting the idea that 'the Eucharist [is] the flesh of our Saviour Jesus Christ, which suffered for our sins'. The term is seen in other second-century texts such as *The Martyrdom of Polycarp*, an account of the burning to death in 155 of a revered Christian leader by Romans in front of a crowd because he refused to renounce his religion, and again in the 'Muratorian Fragment', believed to be the earliest surviving list of the books of the New Testament, dating back to 177.

Catholicism as a state religion

As the far-flung Roman Empire came under sustained attack by barbarian forces in the fourth century, successive imperial leaders tried to scapegoat Christians as the root of the trouble.

Emperor Diocletian in 303, for example, ordered all Christian places of worship to be laid to waste and their holy books burnt. But it was a losing fight for the soul of the empire and in 312 Constantine attributed his latest victory in battle to the Christian god. The age of persecution was over. Constantine's subsequent generosity towards the Catholic Church saw state patronage make possible the first appearance of mighty basilicas in Rome, including that at St John Lateran, the mother church of the city, and until 1308 home to the popes.

Spotlight

According to legend, Constantine's beloved mother, Helena, travelled to Jerusalem and ordered the demolition of the Roman temple that had been built on the site of Jesus' crucifixion. In subsequent excavations, she is said to have found the remains of the 'true cross'. Her son built the church of the Holy Sepulchre on this site.

It was as 'Catholic Christians' that Jesus' followers entered Roman imperial law when Theodosius I (379–95) designated the name for adherents of 'that religion which was delivered to the Romans by the divine Apostle Peter, as it has been preserved by faithful tradition and which is now professed by the Pontiff [Pope] Damasus'. This law, dated 380, established Catholic Christianity as the official religion of the Roman Empire.

With acceptance as part of the state came the opportunity for Catholicism to play a greater and more open role in the community. There were visible places of worship, with a standardized liturgy – an early and immediately recognizable form of the Mass, a term used from the fifth century onwards. A liturgical calendar of feast days was established, with emphasis placed on Christmas, marking the birth of Jesus, and especially on Easter when his death and resurrection were commemorated. Also, the seven sacraments began to be consolidated, in a process not wholly completed until the early Middle Ages.

By the end of the fourth century, Christianity was the religion of the majority of Roman citizens, but the Empire itself was collapsing. As it did, the Church stepped into the vacuum, assuming temporal as well as spiritual authority. Bishops, for example, took charge of the care of the poor in their cities, and came to be seen as the most powerful individuals within the city walls, building a new social order out of the wreckage of the Empire.

Key idea

By linking Church and State, in the wake of the collapse of the Empire, Roman Catholicism proved more enduring than, for example, the earlier Christian communities in the Middle East, which declined to compromise with political rulers.

The growth of papal power

Pope Leo the Great (440–61) is best remembered for his insistence on the supreme authority of the papacy in the Church, moving Catholicism from a system of largely autonomous prelates and bishops, widely scattered about the lands of the old Empire, to the hierarchical model of governance known today. But, under Leo, Christianity also grew in influence and importance in the secular sphere. In 452, as Pope, he confronted Attila the Hun (then laying waste to northern Italy and preparing to head south towards Rome) and persuaded him to withdraw.

'Behold, thanks to Peter, you have become head of the world; you reign over a vaster empire by virtue of divine religion than you ever did by earthly supremacy.'
Pope Leo the Great addressing his fellow Romans

Such a success did not endure and Rome faced wave after wave of invaders. The Emperor was now based in Constantinople in the East, with only an exarch at Ravenna, on the eastern Adriatic coast of Italy, representing imperial power in the West. In Rome, the popes assumed command of the city and surrounding lands, a situation that was to endure for almost 1,400 years.

Among the civil administrators of the city from 572 to 574 was Gregory, who came of a local noble family that had already provided two popes. Gregory (*c.*540–604) abandoned all worldly goods on the death of his father and adopted the new monastic style of life. This had been growing in influence all across the Catholic Church in imitation of the 'Desert Fathers', hermits and ascetics such as Saint Antony (*c.*251–356) who from the third century onwards dedicated their lives to prayer and hard manual labour in loosely knit communities in the Egyptian desert.

Their example inspired others, like Benedict of Nursia (480–547), whose 'Rule' led to the foundation of monasteries in Italy and eventually throughout Europe. These institutions housed men following regimented, celibate lives of prayer, service and learning, and earned widespread public respect. Fiercely loyal to the papacy, the new generation of monks were key figures in extending the Pope's authority.

Gregory was summoned out of his monastery in 590 and elected, by popular acclaim of Roman citizens, as the new Pope. The first monk-pope, he is the second of the popes known by the title 'the Great'. His lasting achievements in the history of Catholicism were fourfold:

1 He firmly established the papacy as the key political power in Rome and central Italy.

2 He insisted that his word, as Pope, took precedence throughout the Western Christian Church (there were still patriarchs – or leaders – with much independence in Antioch, Constantinople, Alexandria and Jerusalem). 'I know of no bishop who is not subject to the Apostolic See when fault has been committed,' Gregory wrote.

3 He was vigorous in sending out his fellow monks as missionaries to modern-day Germany, France and Scandinavia to convert pagans to Catholicism. His envoys included Augustine of Canterbury who, in 597, arrived in England and converted King Ethelbert of Kent.

4 In his many writings on theology and spirituality, such as his *Dialogues*, he summarized the basis for Christian thought in a way that remained popular up to the medieval period.

Spotlight

An eye-catching story told by the eighth-century monk and ecclesiastical historian Bede is that the sight of fair-haired Saxon slaves from Britain in a Roman slave market inspired Pope Gregory to send Augustine to England to try to convert their people. However, it seems likely that practical concerns, such as the spread of papal authority, were more influential.

To the foundations of power, authority and belief that Gregory and his successors had laid, Pope Stephen II (752–7), another scion of a Roman aristocratic family, added a final vital element. In 753 he crossed the Alps to forge an alliance with the Frankish King Pepin. In return for the papal blessing, Pepin granted the papacy political control of much of central Italy, and guaranteed it with his own army. When Pepin's son, Charlemagne, managed to establish his own rule over the European lands that had once constituted the western part of the Roman Empire, he came to Rome in 800 and knelt before Pope Leo III (795–816) to be 'crowned by God' as Holy Roman Emperor. The alliance of the Catholic Church with earthly rulers that was to dominate Europe was now firmly established.

Key thinkers in the first millennium of Catholicism

Along with Pope Gregory the Great, Catholicism hails three other figures among the Fathers of the Church in its first millennium as 'doctors' or great teachers:

1 **Saint Ambrose** (334–97). A Roman governor who was elected Bishop of Milan in 374 by popular acclaim, Ambrose faced down heresy within the Church and forced the emperor Theodosius I to do public penance for ordering a massacre of rioters, insisting that 'the Emperor is within the Church: he is not above it'. His principal legacy, though, was his collected sermons: practical guidelines to believers on the sacraments of baptism, Eucharist and confirmation. A keen advocate of church music, he is credited with introducing it into liturgy.

2 **Saint Augustine of Hippo** (354–430). Baptized a Christian, Augustine drifted away from the Church as a young man and led a worldly and debauched life. However, in 387 he was inspired to return by Ambrose, among others, and served for the rest of his years as an outstanding and admired bishop and teacher in North Africa. His writings – particularly his *Confessions* and *The City of God* – ensured him a central place in Catholicism thereafter, and are still regularly quoted by popes and bishops. Drawing on his own past, Augustine dwelt at length on the sinfulness of human flesh and the dangers for the spirit of human sexuality. His legacy can be seen in Catholicism's distinctive teachings on sex and, some of his critics argue, in its negative attitudes to women.

> 'You have made us for Yourself, and our hearts are restless until they find their rest in You.'
>
> Saint Augustine on God's plan in *Confessions*

3 **Saint Jerome** (342–420). A one-time hermit who travelled extensively, spending time in Antioch, Bethlehem and Constantinople, Jerome was secretary to Pope Damasus I (366–84) and was commissioned by him to translate the gospel texts from Greek into Latin. This task then grew into compiling the whole of the Bible in Latin in his Vulgate (i.e. the vulgar tongue, the scriptures made accessible in the language of the people), completed only in 404. The preeminent biblical scholar in Catholicism, often represented by the figure of a lion, Jerome also contributed through his letters and polemical writings to emerging ideas on doctrine.

Dig deeper

Paul Johnson, *A History of Christianity* (Penguin, 1990).

Edward Stourton, *In the Footsteps of Saint Paul* (Hodder, 2004).

Gary Wills, *Saint Augustine* (Weidenfeld, 1999).

A.N. Wilson, *Paul: The Mind of the Apostle* (Sinclair-Stevenson, 1997).

Fact-check

1 What does 'catholic' mean?
   a   Christian
   b   Founded by Jesus
   c   Universal
   d   Merciful

2 Where, according to the New Testament, was the term 'Christian' first heard?
   a   Antioch
   b   Jerusalem
   c   Nazareth
   d   Ephesus

3 What is the date of the earliest use in writing of the expression 'Catholic Church'?
   a   In John's gospel
   b   In the Acts of the Apostles
   c   In the writings of Saint Augustine
   d   In the writings of Ignatius of Antioch

4 What is the statement of core Church beliefs, agreed in 325, known as?
   a   The Our Father
   b   The Nicene Creed
   c   The Eucharistic Prayer
   d   The Sanctus

5 How did the early Church Father Tertullian refer to the blood split by the martyrs at the hands of their Roman persecutors?
   a   A crime
   b   The work of the Devil
   c   An echo of Jesus' sacrifice
   d   The seed of a new Church

6 How were the first ministers of the Church ordained?
   a   By papal decree
   b   With holy water
   c   By laying on of hands
   d   By reciting a prayer

7 Which Roman Emperor finally ended the Roman persecution of the Christians in 312?

   a Constantine

   b Nero

   c Julius Caesar

   d Diocletian

8 When was 'Catholic Christianity' declared the official religion of the Roman Empire?

   a 312

   b 350

   c 380

   d 425

9 What were the hermit monks called who in the third century lived in the wilds of Sinai and inspired Catholic monasticism?

   a Benedictines

   b Essenes

   c The Egyptian Fathers

   d The Desert Fathers

10 Who was the first monk-pope?

   a Leo the Great

   b Gregory the Great

   c Benedict

   d Damasus

From the Dark Ages to the Reformation

In this chapter you will learn:

▶ *how the popes came to dominate Europe*
▶ *about the role of the Inquisition*
▶ *about the abuses that precipitated the Reformation.*

The history of the Catholic Church, and in particular the history of the papacy, is a tale of peaks and troughs of power and influence in an ever-shifting and often all-absorbing relationship with secular authorities. The link between Church and state, symbolized by Pope Leo III placing the imperial crown on Charlemagne's head in the name of God, became a key factor both in world history and in the story of Catholicism.

The rise to European domination

'My task, assisted by divine piety is everywhere to defend the Church of Christ. Your task, Holy Father, is to raise your hands to God like Moses to ensure the victory of our arms.'
Emperor Charlemagne in a letter to Pope Leo III in 795

The crowning of Charlemagne by Pope Leo marked a high point for the alliance of Church and state that was at the heart of the new Holy Roman Empire. Charlemagne's heirs, however, lacked his gifts as a politician and warrior and ended up fighting among themselves. The Empire collapsed.

The papacy, too, went into decline in the ninth century, a period known in history as the Dark Ages. The successors to Saint Peter abandoned their ambition to rule a Europe-wide Church and concentrated instead only on Rome. They were chosen by and from local Roman families who wanted popes capable of governing their unruly and corrupt city.

Key idea

Confronted by stories of debauched or 'bad' popes, Catholicism stresses that it is the office of the Pope that is important, not the individual holders of it. Their human failings cannot, it says, detract from the papacy's God-given mission.

One particular low point in this period was the legendary election of a German woman of English descent called Joan, disguised as a man, to the papal throne in 853. Another was the subjugation of the office of Pope to the ambitions of a ruthless and immoral Roman matriarch, Marozia, who installed a succession of her lovers and offspring on St Peter's throne during the tenth century, in an era later characterized as a 'pornocracy'.

Case study: Was there ever a Pope Joan?

The story of the 'She-Pope' is recorded by some 500 chroniclers of the papacy, from the twelfth century until the end of the seventeenth century. The authors include several papal servants and bishops, but none was an eyewitness nor even a near-contemporary of Pope John VIII (853–5).

One of the most distinguished of the chroniclers, Martin of Poland, writing in 1277, states that John was excluded from 'the catalogue of holy popes, as well on account of her female sex as on account of the foul nature of the transaction'. John was, in fact, Martin of Poland recounts, a learned German woman and the child of English missionaries, who had first disguised herself as a monk to continue her education, but who had been so successful that she had attracted the patronage of Pope Leo IV and been elected his successor by popular acclaim.

Her gender was discovered only when she fell pregnant and gave birth in the street when travelling from the Lateran Palace, then the home of popes, to the Vatican. The accounts variously describe her as being stoned to death, along with her baby, or tied to the legs of a horse and dragged through the street until dead.

The legend was an accepted, if never celebrated, part of Catholic tradition until the Reformation when, faced by dissidents using it to damn all claims of papal authority, the Catholic Church dismissed Pope Joan as the invention of Protestant forgers. However, the story has lived on, in fiction, art and feminist readings of history.

The evidence for a Pope Joan is intriguing, though not conclusive. It is given wider significance in Catholicism for two reasons. First, Catholicism continues to ban women from the priesthood, though as someone who tricked her way into the papacy Joan is arguably not the best role model for would-be women priests. And second, because it claims that all popes stand in a direct line back to Saint Peter, the Catholic Church regards the story of Joan as tarnishing the 'apostolic succession'.

In conflict with ambitious princes

One of Marozia's descendants, the dissolute John XII (Pope 955–64), elected at the age of just 18, was Pope at the time when Charlemagne's empire underwent a revival under the Saxon leader Otto the Great (912–73). Otto first forced John to crown him Holy Roman Emperor in 962 and then demonstrated his dominance over a weakened papacy by deposing him. This remained a pattern in Catholicism for the next 100 years. Any pope who showed any independence – such as Benedict IX (1032–48) – risked being supplanted by imperial whim with nominees who are now usually described by Catholicism as 'anti-popes'.

Key idea

The relationships and rivalries between popes and secular leaders are part of the story of Catholicism and of the story of Europe. Popes have always been leaders in wider society as well as leaders within the Church itself.

The papacy lost any effective control over who became bishops. 'Lay investiture' – selection of local Church leaders by the Emperor or princes – became a symbol of the papacy's subjugation. With political weakness went moral decline. There was a thriving trade in spiritual goods – up to and including appointment as a bishop or papal servant – that is known as simony, as well as a general lack of discipline among the clergy in both public and private matters. Priests would marry and then discard wives, while their children would lay claim to Church lands. Even the revered monastic movement fell into disrepute.

Key idea

For the first thousand years of Catholicism married priests were the norm, though there was an admired minority who chose to remain celibate.

From the mid-eleventh century onwards, however, Catholicism started to put its house in order. There was a growing move towards enforcing celibacy on all priests – as a way, in part, of avoiding their descendants claiming Church lands. Monastic reforms were epitomized by Bernard of Clairvaux (1090–1153), who advocated a more primitive form of monastic observance. And the papacy began to reassert its independence and win back its place as the equal of temporal rulers, even coming to dominate them. A Church decree of 1059 officially excluded both the Emperor and Roman nobles from any role in electing a new pope, but it fell to Pope Gregory VII (1073–85) to enforce this.

> 'The Pope can be judged by no one; the Roman Church has never erred and will never err till the end of time; the Roman Church was founded by Christ alone; the Pope alone can depose and restore bishops; he alone can make new laws.'
>
> Pope Gregory VII, writing in the *Dictatus Papae* ('The Pope's Memorandum') in 1075

Gregory gave his stated ambition to supreme authority practical expression by standing up to the emperor Henry IV over appointments, excommunicating him (throwing him out of the Church) when he refused to accept the Pope's wishes, and then embarking on a long war with Henry that left Rome in ruins. The battle had not been won by the time of Gregory's death. Indeed, he was in exile from Rome, but under Urban II (1088–99) victory was completed.

Schism with the East

Alongside curbing the influence of outsiders in the running of the Catholic Church, the papacy in this period also reasserted its supreme authority internally. Leo IX (1048–54) was a key figure in this restoration, using tours, councils and writings to impose his beliefs on his Church and bishops, and to clamp down on corruption. The loyalty of the reinvigorated monastic orders considerably strengthened the papacy's hand over any local prelates with independent ideas, while the wiping out of the Christian Church in North Africa – traditionally resistant to Roman dictate – by the rapid spread of Islam along the southern coast of the Mediterranean had the by-product of removing another obstacle to papal ambitions. The ancient patriarchates of Antioch, Alexandria and Jerusalem all fell into decline.

Spotlight

Islam spread all the way to Spain where, in 711, the Muslim Caliphate conquered most of the Iberian Peninsula. The tenth and eleventh centuries of this Moorish Islamic kingdom are regarded as a golden age in Islam. It was gradually eroded until, in 1492, the Catholic monarchs Isabella of Castile and Ferdinand of Aragon finally defeated the Moors in the south of Spain.

The Pope in Rome now had only one internal rival for domination of the universal Catholic Church, the Patriarch of Constantinople. The relationship between Western and Eastern parts of Christianity had long been delicate. There were several schisms, but each was eventually patched up. In the eighth century, for example, there was a dispute between West and East over iconoclasm – Constantinople wished to abolish the use of religious images and Rome objected. Eventually a compromise was found. Each dispute, however, weakened the ties that bound the Eastern Church to the papacy until it seemed content to pay nominal homage to Rome while in practice acting as a self-sufficient and autonomous body.

That tolerance came to an end in the time of Patriarch Michael Cerularius (1043–58). He was impatient with the paramount authority of the papacy, especially when exercised in certain questions concerning the liturgy, and responded by withdrawing permission for the Latin rite of the Western Church to be celebrated in areas under his authority. Pope Leo IX (Pope 1049–54) answered by banning the Greek rite of the Eastern Church in parts of southern Italy ruled by the Byzantine Emperor based in Constantinople.

The dispute escalated, with intemperate papal envoys in Constantinople trying to excommunicate Michael Cerularius. Trust between the Pope and the Patriarch reached a low ebb and remained there when, in 1095, Pope Urban called for a crusade to relieve the pressure Islam was placing on beleaguered Christians in the eastern Mediterranean. When Antioch was retaken in 1098, the Crusaders evicted the Greek Patriarch, loyal to Constantinople, and replaced him with a Latin one, owing his allegiance only to the Pope.

The breach between the two parts of the Catholic family deepened. Matters reached a head during the Fourth Crusade (1202–4), when the Western knights became embroiled in the power struggle of a pretender to the Eastern Emperor's throne. They entered Constantinople and sacked churches there. As a result, Christianity fractured. Attempts were made to heal the wound in 1274 and 1439, but henceforth the Catholic West and the Orthodox East went their own ways.

Key idea

With the break between the Orthodox East and the Catholic West, icons ceased to have any great place in Catholic worship.

Innocent III – the Vicar of Christ

'Just as the founder of the universe established two great lights in the firmament of heaven, the greater light to rule the day and the lesser light to rule the night, so too He set two great dignities in the firmament of the universal church…, the greater on to rule the day, that is, souls, and the lesser to rule the night, that is, bodies. These dignities are the papal authority and the royal power. Now just as the moon derives its light from the sun and is indeed lower than it in quantity and quality, in position and in power, so too the royal power derives the splendour of its dignity from the pontifical authority.'

Pope Innocent III in an 1198 letter to the nobles of Tuscany

Arguably the most ambitious of the papal monarchs was Innocent III (1198–1216). He was the first Pope to describe himself as 'the Vicar of Christ', someone, as he put it, who 'sat midway between God and man, below God but above man'. This person – the Pope – had, in Innocent's words, 'not only the universal Church but the whole world to govern'. It is a claim still made by today's pontiffs who use the title 'Vicar of Jesus Christ'.

Innocent, however, wanted more than titles. He wished to build a system of morality, centred on himself, that would regulate the whole gamut of human behaviour across the known world. This ambition prompted a huge growth in the range and use of Canon – or Church – Law, in an effort to define precisely how each and every Catholic ought to live their life. In 1215 Innocent summoned the Fourth Council of the Lateran, which established such enduring Catholic practices as the obligation to attend the sacraments of confession and Eucharist at least once a year, and set out entry qualifications for candidates for the clergy in an attempt to address the abuses of some rogue priests.

It was no good, Innocent realized, telling people what to do if you could not make them obey, so he also strengthened the Curia – or Rome-based Church bureaucracy – so that it could enforce his writ. He also promoted the system, still in existence in Catholicism today, by which all bishops had to make regular (usually five-yearly) *ad limina* visits to Rome to meet the Pope. The phrase *ad limina* translates as 'to the threshold' and refers to visiting the 'threshold of the Apostles', or the burial place of Saint Peter in Rome. The claim of Apostolic Succession remained at the root of the papacy's authority, notwithstanding the behaviour of some of the popes themselves. It is, however, for commissioning the Inquisition that Innocent is best remembered.

The Inquisition

The Inquisition was established in 1208 as a key instrument of papal government. It consisted of special tribunals charged with rooting out heresy across Europe. Initially, it focused on southern France where the Cathars (or Albigensians), who took their name from the Greek for 'unpolluted', were a group of Catholics living simple, celibate lives. They refused to fall in line with the papacy, regarding Rome as bloated and corrupt. When pressed by Innocent's representative to change their minds, they responded by killing the papal legate.

This killing resulted in the establishment of the Inquisition. Innocent had tired of persuasion and was resorting to coercion. There was nothing in the New Testament to support the methods the Inquisition employed, but he drew on the Old Testament, as well as writers such as Saint Augustine, to justify his innovation. Cathars were tortured – often having their eyes gouged out – in an effort to make them see the sinfulness of their lives. Those who refused (and many who acceded) were killed as 'Devil-worshippers'.

Such was its success in stamping out this particular 'heresy' that, in 1233, the Inquisition was given a permanent place in the Catholic Church. Neither local bishops nor local courts had any power to resist it. Victims were accused on the basis of anonymous denunciations, and seldom had the chance to organize a defence before they were subjected to torture. The activities of the Inquisitors, many of them initially Dominican friars, demonstrated the Church's claim to a jurisdiction that overruled both state and individual conscience. As its ambitions grew, the Church allowed the Inquisition to target any group that was perceived as standing in the way of complete Catholic hegemony in Europe – be they pagans, Jews or even women. All suffered similar demonization by the Inquisition, creating a reign of terror during which many abuses occurred.

Key idea

While the work of the medieval Inquisition strengthened the power of Catholicism in the Middle Ages, it ultimately weakened its moral authority.

The Spanish Inquisition came later, starting in 1478 and only being swept away in 1808 when Napoleon invaded Spain. It alone claimed over 100,000 victims. It differed from the medieval Inquisition in that it was run by the Spanish Crown, with the papacy on several occasions intervening to urge clemency (and being ignored). In one particularly gruesome form of torture, prisoners' hands would be tied behind their backs and their bodies then hoisted off the ground. They would be left suspended for hours or days until they were ready to 'confess' their sins. In another, the accused would be strapped to a trestle table, with their feet higher than their heads, while the priestly inquisitors would pour water down their throats.

Spotlight

The *Malleus Maleficarum*, sometimes called 'The Hammer of the Witches', was the handbook of the Inquisition. It attempted to explain away every episode of ill-fortune, illness or natural disaster by reference to the activity of Devil-worshipping witches. 'Witchcraft', it states, 'is high treason against God's majesty ... and [the accused] are to be put to torture to make them confess.'

Avignon popes

Innocent's reign marked the high point of papal power in the wider European context. The prince he had hand-picked to become the next Holy Roman Emperor, Frederick II of Sicily (1194–1250), was anything but compliant with papal demands and instead engaged in a long and bitter battle for supremacy with first Gregory IX (1227–41) and then the candidate he had himself chosen as Gregory's successor-but-one, Innocent IV (1243–54).

However, the greatest threat to papal authority over the Church came increasingly not from Germany but from France, where Philip IV 'the Fair' (1268–1314) clashed repeatedly with Pope Boniface VIII (1294–1303), even trying to kidnap the pontiff and bring him to France where he would be forced to abdicate. Boniface avoided this fate, but his successor-but-one, Clement V (1305–14), did not share his resilience and bowed to Philip's demand to relocate himself, and the papacy, to Avignon in southern France. He was the first of seven 'Avignon popes', leading the Church between 1305 and 1378 but, in practice, subjugating it to the French monarchy.

When the papacy finally managed to return to Rome, urged on by figures such as Catherine of Siena (1347–80), and reassert its independence, it was immediately plunged into the Forty-Year Schism with the election of the unstable and tyrannical Urban VI in 1378. By now there was a group of senior churchmen, known as cardinals, who were able to exert influence on the Pope from within the Church. The first cardinals had existed in ninth-century Rome, as heads of the city's most important churches, but by the twelfth century they had spread throughout the Catholic world. Among their powers was that of electing the Pope.

Key idea

There were no cardinals in Catholicism until the ninth century. Their leading role in the election of popes started only in the twelfth century.

After Urban had demonstrated his autocratic tendencies, the cardinals were split. Some felt they had no choice but to follow the man they had elected. An opposing group appealed to the French monarch for support in deposing Urban in favour of Clement VII, a candidate more to their taste. Both groups refused to back down, so there were two popes – one in Rome and one in Avignon. In 1409 the cardinals held a council at Pisa and agreed to depose both ruling popes and replace them with an alternative, Alexander V. However, the two incumbents refused to go and, as Alexander was now in office, Catholicism had three popes.

The matter was finally solved at the Council of Constance in 1414. All three popes were removed in favour of Martin V, a candidate acceptable to all parties. Part of the compromise was the imposition on the Church of a more collective style of leadership, with popes directed to consult with their cardinals on the crucial questions of reform that were facing Catholicism.

Corruption, simony, high ecclesiastical taxes and the debacle of having three popes simultaneously had all sapped the Church's authority. Yet, rather than attack the root causes, popes and cardinals preferred to indulge in a running battle for authority that was never quite resolved. It left the Church weakened as it faced new threats after the Ottoman Turks had taken Constantinople in 1453 and began advancing into Europe.

Thomas Aquinas

Saint Thomas Aquinas (1225–74) is regarded by many as the greatest of all Catholic theologians. Educated by the Benedictines in Italy, he became a Dominican friar. Aquinas was convinced that faith and reason were compatible. 'For the knowledge of any truth whatsoever,' he wrote, 'man needs divine help, that the intellect may be moved by God to its act.' To prove the point, he returned to the philosophers of ancient Greece, notably Aristotle (384–322 BC), and borrowed from their ideas to create a rational understanding of God as the creator and source of all being, goodness and truth, who is present in us all.

> 'Saint Thomas exalted God without lowering Man; he exalted Man without lowering Nature. Therefore, he made a cosmos of common sense; terra viventium; a land of the living. His philosophy, like his theology, is that of common sense.'
>
> The Catholic novelist G.K. Chesterton, writing in 1932

Aquinas left as his most significant gift to the Church the *Summa Theologia* (1266–74), a systematic exposition of theology, based on reason, which earned him the title 'universal teacher'. He described four kinds of law: eternal, natural, human and divine. Eternal law is the decree of God that governs all creation. Natural law is the human 'participation' in the eternal law and is discovered by reason. Natural law ensures that 'good is to be done and promoted, and evil is to be avoided'. This belief in a preordained, moral pattern of behaviour, learned by observing (as Aquinas had) the behaviour of animals, continues to guide Catholic attitudes. Still influential is his defence of priestly celibacy – 'the state of virginity is preferable to that of even continent marriage'.

Impression of power

In the late fifteenth century the Renaissance papacy gave every outward impression of being more powerful than ever. The show of wealth, the commissioning of great works of art that are part of the Catholic treasury to this day, and the flamboyant lifestyles of some popes suggested an institution in rude health. The reality, however, was that Catholicism was in moral and spiritual decline. Political power and personal gain mattered more to Church leaders than principles. Alexander VI (1492–1503), sometimes called the 'Borgia Pope', was, for example, installed as Pope with his various children looking on.

Despairing of Rome and the papacy, there were many local reform movements that aimed at restoring the public esteem of the clergy, recapturing the high ideals of the monasteries, and even empowering the laity – such as the brotherhood founded in 1497 in Genoa by Ettore Vernazza and known as the Oratory of Divine Love. It sought spiritual renewal by dedication to prayer, meditation and acts of charity, and spread to Rome, Naples and Bologna.

None, however, was sufficient to turn back the outbreak of dissatisfaction that was to divide Christianity. When an Augustinian monk and teacher, Martin Luther (1483–1546), questioned the corruption and the simony, his attack precipitated a wider crisis. There was a theological basis to Luther's rebellion. He rejected the notion, central to Catholicism then and now, that by doing good works you could earn salvation after death. Such an idea, Luther felt, was simply an invitation to ego. Salvation came through faith in God. It was not an individual's holiness that counted. It was God's love.

Luther's criticism broadened to take in other aspects of Catholicism. He emphasized the importance of a personal relationship with God, rather than one conducted through the intermediary of a priest, and he constantly referred to the Bible rather than to the traditional practices and interpretations of the Church. However, his position was not so very far from Catholicism on many subjects that he inevitably had to cause a schism. It was the context in which he launched his onslaught that led to that.

His programme – according to legend, set out in the 95 theses he nailed to the door of the castle church in Wittenberg in October 1517, but more likely to have been contained in a letter he sent to his bishop, and then circulated when he received no reply – certainly had a popular appeal. His attack in particular on the sale of indulgences – the idea that if you paid the Church money, it could mitigate your sins, or those of friends and relatives already dead and awaiting God's final judgement – struck a chord with all those who felt the Church had grown corrupt in linking financial and spiritual matters. Indulgences were sold, for example, to fund the building of a new St Peter's Basilica, finally started in 1608.

The theses of Martin Luther

Four of the 95 Theses

1 The true treasure of the Church is the Most Holy Gospel of the glory and the grace of God.
2 To think the papal pardons so great that they could absolve a man even if he had committed an impossible sin and violated the Mother of God – this is madness.
3 To say that the cross, emblazoned with the papal arms, is of equal worth with the Cross of Christ is blasphemy.
4 Why does not the Pope, whose wealth is today greater than the riches of the richest, build just one church of St Peter with his own money, rather than with the money of poor believers?

Luther was also an adept orator, who used advances in printing techniques to get his message to a wide audience. He was treated far too casually at first by an arrogant papacy and its bishops. They began by dismissing his protests, unable to see that he was speaking for a large constituency. Then, when Rome felt Luther needed to be answered, it produced a response, in 1520, that was widely condemned as vague, weak and full of personal invective.

Rome also failed to see that Luther's revolt could be exploited by princes who – however sincerely they may have agreed or disagreed with what he was saying – saw an opportunity to curtail the power and claims of the papacy over their domains. The protection offered by Frederick, the Elector of Saxony, ensured that Luther didn't end up silenced or killed by the Inquisition.

As Luther's popularity grew, he was emboldened to extend his attack into a full-scale assault on the papacy and the whole concept of the Apostolic Succession. He also rejected five of the seven sacraments, limiting himself to baptism and Eucharist (with the notion of transubstantiation tempered), and advocated a pared-down liturgy delivered not in Latin but in the local language so as to make it accessible.

Summoned by Charles V, the Holy Roman Emperor (1500–58), before the Diet (assembly) of Worms in 1521, Luther refused to recant because my 'conscience is held captive to the Word of God'. The Emperor, who had vowed to stamp out heresy, was prevented by the German princes from acting decisively against Luther. Again their motives were both spiritual and political. The new Lutheranism was taken up in some German cities. Catholic Christendom was once more divided.

At first it was believed to be a temporary division, but the structures of Lutheranism grew quickly, especially in the absence of the Emperor who was heavily involved in affairs in Spain from 1521 to 1530. The best chance at reconciliation came in 1541 at Regensburg, based on conceding to the Lutherans (also known as Protestants) a married clergy and freedom from papal jurisdiction while still recognizing papal primacy, but Rome could not agree to give so much ground.

Spotlight

Luther did not reject all of his Catholic heritage. He remained, for example, acutely conscious of the threat posed by the Devil. Luther's belief in Satan was such that he ascribed his own problems with indigestion and stomach-ache to the Devil's having possessed his bowels.

Luther's ideas therefore spread across Europe and inspired a variety of reformed or Protestant Churches to spring up. In England, Henry VIII (1491–1547), hitherto a staunch supporter of the papacy, embraced the new Protestant spirit to resolve a dispute over divorcing his first wife and marrying Anne Boleyn, as part of his determination to have a male heir. Subsequent English monarchs swung between extreme Protestantism – Edward VI (1537–53) – and aggressive Catholicism – Mary I (1516–58) – until Elizabeth (1533–1603) built a consensus around a moderate form of Protestantism in the Church of England, retaining such aspects of Catholicism as bishops.

Conclusion

The high-water mark of Catholic influence in Europe had been reached. Its political ambitions had weakened the papacy's moral authority, and its intolerance of dissent had cost it dearly. The Reformation finally destroyed the outward show of unity that bound together Catholic Europe. It was as much a political as a theological revolution. Henceforth, the Catholic Church would be one among several branches of the Christian family.

Dig deeper

Patrick Collinson, *The Reformation* (Weidenfeld & Nicolson, 2003).

Eamon Duffy, *Ten Popes Who Shook the World* (Yale University Press, 2011).

Toby Green, *Inquisition* (Macmillan, 2007).

Richard Marius, *Martin Luther: The Christian between God and Death* (Harvard University Press, 2000).

The Venerable Bede, *The Ecclesiastical History of the English People* (Oxford University Press, 1999).

Fact-check

1 Which of the following is true of priests in the first 1,000 years of Catholicism?
   a All were obliged to be celibate
   b All were married
   c Most were married
   d Most were women

2 In what position did Bernard of Clairvaux play a reforming role in Catholicism in the twelfth century?
   a As Pope
   b As a bishop
   c As a cardinal
   d As a monk

3 When he appointed bishops, whom did Pope Gregory VII consult before making his decision?
   a No one else
   b The local prince or king
   c The local clergy
   d Local Catholics

4 In the eighth century, what did the Western and Eastern parts of the Church fall out over?
   a Money
   b Icons
   c The Crusades
   d The Bible

5 Who was the first pope to call himself 'the Vicar of Christ'?
   a John Paul II
   b Gregory VIII
   c Innocent III
   d Leo III

6 In 1215, at the Fourth Lateran Council, with what frequency were Catholics told to go to confession and the Eucharist?
   a At least seven times a year
   b At least once a week
   c At least once a month
   d At least once a year

7 What is the Curia?
  a The Vatican administration
  b A church hospital
  c A miracle cure
  d A bishop's throne

8 Who makes *ad limina* visits to the Pope?
  a Priests
  b Kings
  c Bishops
  d Theologians

9 In the fourteenth century the papacy operated in exile from which French city?
  a Paris
  b Amiens
  c Avignon
  d Aix-en-Provence

10 Who established the theory of natural law?
  a Thomas More
  b Thomas Aquinas
  c Thomas à Becket
  d Erasmus

Counter-Reformation to Holocaust

In this chapter you will learn:

▶ *how Catholicism recovered from the Reformation*

▶ *how it was attacked by Enlightenment thinkers*

▶ *how it retreated from the modern world.*

In the years after Luther's revolt, over half of Europe's believers, according to some documents, turned their back on Rome. It was the greatest crisis ever to face the Catholic Church and its leaders. The result could simply have been that Catholicism withered on the vine. Instead it came back renewed and refocused, with a cautious, traditional and often deeply suspicious view of the world in which it operated.

The Counter-Reformation

Not everything that happened in the Catholic Church after the Reformation can be put down to a reaction against Luther. There were already areas of new growth that pre-dated 1517, often small groups, or brotherhoods, dedicated to cleansing the priesthood and encouraging better administration of the Church. It is in such groups that we find the origins of the Jesuits, started by the Spaniard Ignatius Loyola (1491–1556) in Paris in 1534 and granted papal approval in 1540.

> 'There is no doubt the Jesuits are the real men of Rome – i.e. we fall in with none others. I don't mean to say how great they are, but only they are the prominent men.'
> Convert English Catholic cardinal Blessed John Henry Newman, writing in 1846

In the Reformation era, too, can be seen the roots of the Capuchins, an offshoot of the Franciscans, aiming to return the order to its original goals, and founded in 1528. They were soon a familiar sight with their coarse robes and large square hoods. These two groups – Jesuits and Capuchins – were among the leaders of the Counter-Reformation.

Spotlight

Pope Francis is the first Jesuit ever elected as Pope. He was provincial (or head) of the Jesuits in his native Argentina in the 1970s.

The fight-back began in December 1545 with the opening of a council in the northern Italian city of Trento (in English, Trent).

The actual meetings took no more than three years, but were spread out over 18 years while the new programme was agreed. Consensus was finally reached in 1563 and the Council of Trent addressed head-on some of Luther's most damaging accusations:

1 It restated the Catholic belief that both scripture and tradition play their parts in shaping faith and a moral life.

2 It rejected the notion of justification by faith alone, and insisted on the need for hope and charity, especially in the form of good works.

3 It maintained that the seven sacraments – not just two – all had divine validity.

4 It insisted that henceforth all those wanting to be priests should be celibate, and should be trained according to strict and strictly enforced central rules in seminaries, run by local bishops.

5 It endorsed the hierarchical model of the Church, with the Pope wielding supreme authority and local bishops controlling their diocese, priests and laity.

6 It reformed the Mass, leading to the issuing in 1570 of the *Missale Romanum* – the Roman Missal which held sway until the 1960s – with a rigid liturgical formula, to be followed everywhere and known as the Tridentine rite.

Spotlight

The Tridentine rite has survived, despite the efforts of Catholic reformers to consign it to history. In the 1970s and 1980s its use was severely restricted, lest loyalty to it detract from the new liturgical arrangements. It has since been made more widely available, for the small minority of Catholics, many of them elderly, who still regard it with affection.

There had, of course, been reforming councils in the past. The test of Trent was not its ambitions, but how effectively they were implemented. The post-Reformation papacy was blessed in this regard by figures like Pius V (1566–72), a morally upright, monkish former Inquisitor, who rooted out corruption in the Curia and led by personal example. He promoted his *Catechism* as a basic guide to the good Catholic life, revived the Inquisition (which had been in decline outside Spain) as a way of maintaining discipline, and in 1571 produced an *Index of Condemned Books* to guide Catholic readers away from texts likely to corrupt them.

> **Key idea**
>
> The Council of Trent was a crucial moment in building the future of Catholicism after the earthquake of the Reformation.

The successes of the Counter-Reformation were not simply down to one man, however. A generation of energetic bishops in their dioceses spearheaded the strengthening of Catholicism at local level, ably assisted by the Capuchins, Jesuits and other religious orders. Loyola's *Spiritual Exercises* – a vigorous combination of inner prayer and spirituality with external hard work and determination – inspired not just his followers but many others throughout the Church and continues to do so to this day. Taking seriously Trent's commitment to good works playing their part in faith, the Jesuits and other religious orders took up the challenge with gusto to care for the poor, run schools, encourage learning through universities, and export the faith as missionaries to the 'New World' that had opened up following the American discoveries of Christopher Columbus after 1492. It was a Jesuit, Francis Xavier (1506–52), who carried Catholicism first to Portuguese India at Goa in 1542 and then to Japan and China.

The net effect of this Counter-Reformation revival was to see Catholicism restored to lands where it had been displaced by the new Protestantism. In Poland, France, the southern Netherlands and parts of Germany, it regained its former influence.

Jansenism and Gallicanism

By the middle of the seventeenth century the immediate post-Reformation map had been redrawn. Catholicism had expanded once again at the expense of Protestantism, but the two sides had reached a stalemate. Henceforth the greatest threats to the Catholic Church came from within, in the form of internal dissidents, and from outside, with the rise of an intellectual movement in the Enlightenment which had little time for traditional religion.

The Catholic bishop Cornelius Jansen of Ypres (1585–1638) preached and wrote at length about the essential corruption of human nature. His pessimistic view of human sinfulness, rooted in the notion of the inheritance of Original Sin from Adam and Eve, owed much, Jansen admitted, to Saint Augustine of Hippo. The Jesuits, however, saw in Jansen's writings the influence of Protestant thought about humanity being totally subject to God's will. They condemned him and his followers – the Jansenists – with the backing of the papacy and the French Crown.

The involvement of the Pope and the French monarch gave the dispute a wider resonance, with those who disputed papal claims of jurisdiction and political opponents of the king rallying to the Jansenist cause. An essentially theological dispute took on a political dimension. Official condemnation came from Rome, but the clash continued to create divisions, especially in France and the Low Countries.

Also of French origin was Gallicanism, which sought a return to the pre-Reformation pattern of cardinals and Pope jointly running the Church, and therefore rejected Roman centralization and overarching papal claims. A German version of the same movement was known as Febronianism.

Another movement within Catholicism at this time was Ultramontanism. The Ultramontanes rejected Jansenist and Gallican positions, and insisted that every Catholic's main and often only loyalty should be, not to secular authority, local church, or even spiritual conscience, but to the Pope, who was literally 'ultramontane' – over the mountains – in Rome.

Again, those with axes to grind became involved. Louis XIV (1638–1715) gave support to Gallicanism, bringing him into a prolonged and bitter struggle with Pope Innocent XI (1676–89). With the French Bourbons vying with the Habsburgs in Spain and Germany for influence on the political stage of Europe, the papacy in this period often found itself the subject of intrigue between the two ruling families, as each tried to ensure its candidate was elected to Saint Peter's throne. Such machinations served only to weaken the Pope's authority.

That muddled and muddied world of competing secular influences, exploiting internal divisions within Catholicism, played a significant part in the closing down of the Jesuits in 1773. The Society of Jesus – to give Loyola's followers their correct name – had made many enemies in their role as front-line crusaders of the Counter-Reformation, arch defenders of papal influence. When, in the eighteenth century, the Society became involved in financial and political scandals in France and in controversy on account of its social experiments in the New World that angered the Spanish monarchs, their opponents pressed the papacy to take action.

In France, the Jesuits were abolished by royal decree in 1764. They were expelled from Spain in 1767. Pope Clement XIII (1758–69) resisted these moves fiercely but, in the election that followed his death, Bourbon and Habsburg pressure ensured a pope, Clement XIV (1769–74), who soon saw he had no choice but to bow to royal wishes. In 1773 the Jesuits were disbanded.

The Enlightenment

'By the 1780s, every Catholic state in Europe wanted to reduce the Pope to a ceremonial figurehead, and most succeeded.'
Cambridge historian Eamon Duffy in *Saints & Sinners: A History of the Popes* (1997)

The fall of the Jesuits was greeted as a great triumph for Enlightenment thinking. Hitherto, in the history of Catholicism, the most formidable intellectual challenges had come from thinkers within its ranks, some of whom, like Luther, had then left. The growth in Enlightenment thinking from the mid-seventeenth and through the eighteenth century confronted the Church with enemies from without who rejected everything it stood for. Humankind need no longer, the Enlightenment thinkers wrote, feel at odds with their world, under threat and therefore in need of the Church's protection. Events that had, in the past, been attributed to God's intervention in the world were now being explained rationally by a new generation of scientists.

The Enlightenment challenged Catholicism on its home ground – questions of human nature, our place in the universe, history and morality. Europe was experiencing the dawn of secular culture, with its roots not in the Bible or Church tradition, but rather in science and human experience. Catholicism's instinctive and defensive reaction was to condemn. When devout thinkers such as Galileo Galilei (1564–1642) tried to ease the Church into a new world where the earth was no longer the centre of everything, but a sphere travelling around the sun, they were rejected. Galileo was condemned as a heretic in 1633.

Spotlight

Much is said and written now about the clash between religion and science, not least by the English evolutionary biologist Professor Richard Dawkins. His arguments are not new ones. This particular dispute can be traced back to the eighteenth-century Enlightenment.

The new ideas of rationalism, religious freedom and personal autonomy that came with the Enlightenment threatened Catholicism in the same way that its own teachings had once threatened the bedrock of the Roman Empire. They were the antithesis of everything Catholicism held dear. In particular, the Church disliked the optimism about human nature and progress that was part of the Enlightenment. So they lashed out. Voltaire's *Dictionnaire philosophique* of 1764, for example, was ordered to be burnt, in both France and Rome.

The French Revolution

The French Revolution was, in one sense, a product of Enlightenment thinking. Efforts to reform the government of France, to increase popular participation, started with a gathering of representatives at Versailles in the spring of 1789. The French Catholic Church and the papacy were not wholly opposed to such change. Some clergy took part in the assembly and voted for the proposed reforms, but as events gathered momentum and swept away the monarchy and the whole social order, organized religion itself inevitably came under attack. Church lands were confiscated and clergy were required to take an oath of allegiance to the new French republic.

This raised the age-old issue of the Church's relationship with the state. Pope Pius VI (1775–99) ordered the clergy to refuse the oath. He gave his blessing to the coalition of countries gathering to bring down the Revolution and was punished for it when the triumphant French forces under Napoleon Bonaparte invaded the Papal States in 1796.

In February 1798 the French seized Rome and deposed Pius as head of state. He died in exile the following year, but the cardinals, meeting in Venice under Austrian protection, elected Pius VII (1800–23), a more moderate figure, who declared there was no inevitable conflict between Catholicism and democracy. He returned to Rome and in 1801 agreed a concordat with the French, headed by Bonaparte, now first First Counsel, which recognized Catholicism as the religion of the majority of the French. Three years later the Pope travelled to Paris to crown Bonaparte as Emperor, but their accommodation was short-lived. When Napoleon took on the rest of Europe, Pius declared himself neutral. The outraged Emperor retook Rome in 1809 and thereafter held the Pope captive until his defeat in 1815.

Retreat from a changing world

In the peace that followed, Pius emerged with honour for having enraged Bonaparte. As a result, he was able to roll back state incursions on his authority and so reclaim the right to name bishops. Moreover, he was recognized once again as ruler of the Papal States. He even managed to re-establish the Jesuits, with little opposition from governments.

There was a new energy and confidence in Catholicism, but as the century progressed it grew increasingly alarmed by the pace of change in the world and sided with an Old Order that was in decline in the face of liberal, democratic, economic and secular pressures. In the 1820s, though, there were great hopes that a more liberal form of Catholicism would grow, in harmony with the new liberal mood in Europe, especially among the professional middle classes. The leading advocates of such a development were figures like the Breton priest Hugues-Félicité Robert de Lamennais (1782–1854), who argued for the separation of Church and state as a way of freeing Catholicism from the baggage and concerns of the past, and thereby offering the chance to engage more closely with the lives of those in the pews.

Lamennais supported religious freedom, freedom of the press, and universal suffrage, arguing that the Church had nothing to fear and much to gain from such liberal demands. He attracted much popular support but in 1832 was roundly denounced by Pope Gregory XVI (1831–46) in his encyclical *Mirari Vos* – 'On Liberalism and Religious Indifferentism'. Freedom of conscience, Gregory stated, was a form of madness. In liberalism lay the rejection of supernatural revelation.

Key idea

In the nineteenth century Catholicism was usually to be found siding with those political leaders who opposed reform, change and modernization.

Pius IX

When Pius IX was elected Pope in 1846, he was initially hailed as a man who understood and sympathized with the social and political changes afoot in Europe. He played up to the image, freeing political prisoners and extending the franchise in the Papal States. But the revolutions of 1848, which swept through the capitals of Europe, terrified him. He was forced to flee Rome when the Italian nationalist, Giuseppe Garibaldi, seized power there and declared it a republic.

The insurrection was short-lived. Pius was restored in 1850 by French troops, but returned with any liberal notions he had ever held gone. The movement towards a united Italy, growing in strength in the north of the country, was greeted with the Pope's intransigent hostility. Yet by 1860 his earthly domain had shrunk to little more than the city of Rome. With another wave of nationalist uprisings in 1870, it was swept away altogether.

Impotent to halt the political changes in Europe, Pius clung ever more tightly to his teaching authority to wreak a kind of revenge. Symbolic of the siege mentality with which he infected the Catholic Church was his *Syllabus of Errors* of 1864, a condemnation of liberalism and the modern world in all its aspects. The climax of Pius's reign was the First Vatican Council, which gathered in St Peter's Basilica in December 1869, against a backdrop of Italian troops finally claiming Rome as their national capital. It declared the papacy infallible in questions of faith and morality.

Key idea

Catholic teaching has contained an explicit definition of papal infallibility only since 1870.

Case study: Papal infallibility

The cardinals at the First Vatican Council cast their votes for and against papal infallibility while a thunderstorm raged over Rome on 18 July 1870. Many were reluctant to go along with Pius IX's demands. When the measure was passed, the Pope declared victory as lightning flashed. It was, one cardinal observed, like Moses promulgating the law on Mount Sinai.

The strong opposition to the Pope's decision to set down in Catholic law the doctrine of papal infallibility came about because many cardinals feared that Pius IX was attempting to bolster his spiritual authority as a replacement for his lost political control of Rome. Yet most Catholic theologians in the nineteenth century would have supported the idea that, in theory, the Pope could teach infallibly. The danger, however, was being too prescriptive as to when infallibility could apply.

The tradition that the papacy had preserved apostolic truth had clearly become enshrined by 519, when Pope Hormisdas (514–23) produced his 'Formula of Hormisdas', agreed by the Emperor Justin (450–527). This cited Jesus' words to Peter in Matthew's gospel, entrusting him with leadership of the Church, and used them to endorse the primacy of the see of Rome in which the Catholic faith was preserved in its purity.

However, the word 'infallibility' was rarely used. Instead, the concept was more that the office of pope, taken over many years if not centuries, could not err. The debate on infallibility was reignited in the nineteenth century, with traditional Catholic thinkers arguing that, in post-French Revolutionary Europe, the papacy should be the blueprint for all restored monarchies, and that the power of individual popes to speak without error should therefore be publicly acknowledged.

Since 1870, only the 1950 papal declaration concerning the Assumption – that Mary had been assumed body and soul into heaven – has been explicitly defined as infallible teaching.

A new dawn

The intellectual siege that set Catholicism at odds with the world around it was lifted to a degree with the election of Leo XIII (1878–1903). His encyclical *Rerum Novarum* ('Of Revolutionary Change') of 1891, for example, belatedly engaged Catholics with the injustices created by industrialization. This was followed by the rise across Catholic Europe of Christian Democratic parties, with close links with the papacy, which had at their core the Catholic values set out in *Rerum Novarum*.

Key idea

Rerum Novarum is one of the foundation stones for what is today called Catholic social teaching, and shows the Church taking the side of workers against unscrupulous bosses.

The rise of fascism

Catholicism failed to meet the challenge of new scientific thought in the nineteenth century, notably the work of Charles Darwin (1809–82) and his evolutionary view of humankind's origins. Instead Leo XIII retreated into a reaffirmation, in the encyclical *Aeterni Patris* ('Of the Eternal Father', 1879), of the enduring insights contained in the thirteenth-century teachings of Saint Thomas Aquinas. Modernism – both in the secular sense of the workings and concerns of the modern world, and in the Church sense of a progressive theological movement trying to engage with that world – was to be resisted at all costs.

The papacy remained neutral during World War I (1914–18), though Benedict XV (1914–22) made plain his opposition to, and pain at, the conflict. In its aftermath, the Christian Democratic parties of Catholic Europe did not prove sufficiently robust to counter the rise of fascism, especially in Italy and Germany. In Spain, the Catholic Church sided instinctively with the fascist dictator Franco.

Spotlight

The Catholic Church's support for Franco during and after the Spanish Civil War cemented the impression in progressive circles that the Church was their opponent. The Spanish conflict attracted to the Republican side many left-wing intellectuals and trade unionists from across Europe, and those who survived carried with them a distrust of the Church that lasted decades.

The papacy was hindered in responding to events on its doorstep in Italy by its 1929 concordat with the fascist leader Mussolini, which had created the Vatican City State as the Pope's independent domain. In Germany, likewise, Catholicism struggled to provide an adequate opposition to Adolf Hitler. Though some local Catholic bishops and priests realized the danger that he posed, the overall view of the Vatican was that Hitler had to be endured as a bulwark against godless Soviet communism which posed the greatest threat of all to the future of Catholicism.

Pius XI (1922–39) realized the folly of this position in his 1937 encyclical, *Mit brennender Sorge* – the German phrase for 'with great anxiety'. It was a condemnation of Nazism and Hitler, whom it labelled 'a mad prophet possessed of repulsive arrogance'. Yet Pius died just as he was preparing another outspoken attack on the Nazi ideology. His successor, the wartime pope Pius XII (1939–58), decided thereafter to say nothing, a silence on the subject of the Nazi Holocaust of 6 million Jews that has been much criticized subsequently.

Pius XII and wartime 'silence'

The principal charges against Pius XII were:

▶ that he made no public statement of condemnation even when he had firm evidence from 1940 onwards that the Nazis were exterminating millions of Jews

▶ that he was, therefore, anti-Semitic

▶ that he preferred to turn a blind eye to Nazi atrocities because he feared that Hitler was the only alternative to Soviet-style communism sweeping across Europe and destroying the Church

▶ that he believed the welfare of German Catholics was more important than that of Jews, and therefore was not willing to risk Nazi reprisals on Catholics if he spoke out

▶ that he made only some small and inconsistent gestures to help Jews after 1942 when it was clear that Germany was facing defeat, and that his stance was therefore politically motivated, not morally determined

▶ that Vatican diplomats failed to help Jews escape persecution by getting visas to travel to Palestine because the Pope opposed the idea of a Jewish homeland there

▶ that in the immediate post-war period, Pius showed his true colours by allowing the Vatican to be used as a conduit to spirit away Nazi war criminals to Africa and Latin America.

Admirers of Pius XII offer in his defence:

▶ that he was unaware of the true horror of the Holocaust

▶ that he believed he had to maintain a stance of strict neutrality in World War II so as to maintain the independence of the Church and play a part in the eventual peace settlement

▶ that he did make veiled references to the Holocaust in one broadcast, at Christmas 1942, when he spoke out in general terms against 'progressive exterminations'

▶ that he worked behind the scenes with Church organizations to save as many as 5,000 Jews living in Rome from deportation to the death camps

▶ that he intervened in March 1944 behind the scenes to pressure the Hungarian government to cease the deportations of Jews it has agreed to in July 1944.

In response to the international attacks on Pius XII's record, the Vatican agreed in 1999 to establish a joint commission with Jewish historians to research its own archives and present a fuller picture of Pius's role. Two years later the Jewish members of the committee stood down in protest at Rome's refusal to open its archive fully. Rome said that it could not because the sections in question had not yet been catalogued. Meanwhile, the Vatican is pressing on with plans to make Pius XII a saint. In 2009 he was declared Venerable, one step on the way of canonization. The World Jewish Congress labelled the move 'inopportune and premature'. Pope Francis has indicated his support for continuing with the 'process' that would create Saint Pius XII.

Conclusion

The history of Catholicism can read as a history of the actions of popes. In part, this happens because the greatest historical record is of the activities of the papacy, rather than of individual Catholics. However, Catholicism is also a hierarchical organization, a system built in imitation of the Roman Empire. Indeed, the Church replaced that Empire as the single greatest and most enduring political and moral force in Europe. So it is natural that any account of its history will be guided by the activities of its leaders.

Yet, as Catholicism entered the second half of the twentieth century, it was facing a new set of challenges – the unprecedented pace of social, scientific and economic change, a revolution in communications that meant its every action could be held up to scrutiny, and a much greater concentration on the rights of each individual. How it reacted has shaped the Catholic Church of today.

Dig deeper

John Cornwell, *Hitler's Pope* (Viking, 1997).

Daniel Jonah Goldhagen, *A Moral Reckoning* (Little Brown, 2002).

John Pollard, *The Unknown Pope: Benedict XV* (Geoffrey Chapman, 1999).

Edward Stourton, *Absolute Truth: The Catholic Church in the World Today* (Viking, 1998).

Jonathan Wright, *The Jesuits* (HarperCollins, 2004).

Fact-check

1 How many Jesuit popes have there been?
- **a** None
- **b** 1
- **c** 7
- **d** 14

2 What are Ignatius Loyola's famous *Spiritual Exercises*?
- **a** A keep-fit-plan
- **b** A prayer manual
- **c** His autobiography
- **d** A guide to inner and outer spiritual health

3 According to Gallicanism, with whom did final authority in the Church lie?
- **a** The Pope
- **b** The people of God
- **c** The Pope and bishops jointly
- **d** The bishops

4 According to the Ultramontanes, to whom or what did Catholics have primary loyalty?
- **a** Their local priest
- **b** The Scriptures
- **c** Their bishop
- **d** The Pope?

5 When were the Jesuits disbanded by the Pope?
- **a** 1773
- **b** 1783
- **c** 1789
- **d** Never

6 What did Pius IX's *Syllabus of Errors* condemn?
- **a** Bad spelling
- **b** Liberalism
- **c** Fascism
- **d** The Holocaust

7 Papal infallibility became the official doctrine of the Church in
  a The first century
  b Under Pope Leo the Great
  c At the Council of Trent
  d In 1870

8 What does the 1891 papal encyclical *Rerum Novarum* champion?
  a Workers' rights
  b Papal infallibility
  c Capitalism
  d Communism

9 How might the the official Vatican position during World War I be best described?
  a Pro-German
  b Pro-British
  c As neutral
  d It was unstated

10 When was the Vatican City State established as an independent country?
  a 1928
  b 1929
  c 1930
  d 1933

Part Three

The Catholic Church today

The modern Catholic Church

In this chapter you will learn:

► *about the Second Vatican Council*
► *how the Church divided over contraception*
► *about the life and legacy of John Paul II.*

'The [Second Vatican] Council was a beautiful work of the Holy Spirit. Think of Pope John: he seemed a good pastor, and he was obedient to the Holy Spirit, and he did that.'

Pope Francis in a homily in April 2013

To those who participated in or watched closely its discussions, the Second Vatican Council, which took place between 1962 and 1965, was an exhilarating, intoxicating time that shaped their faith and practice ever after. It was a reappraisal and reform of almost every significant aspect of the Church and its teaching – and this in an organization that says it never changes its mind. The decisions reached by the Council Fathers – the bishops from all around the world who met in Rome – have shaped Catholicism ever since in a direct and everyday way. Some have become so much a part of Catholic life that they go unquestioned, while others remain controversial.

Key idea

Today's Catholic Church is heavily influenced by the decisions of the Second Vatican Council.

Many Catholics, in the Council and post-Council era, have been forced to adjust from the moral certainties of old to a new world where there is not always a wholly satisfying answer to every question. Often, there are many answers and Catholics have struggled to make sense of it all. The debate, discussion and dissent this has caused have, for many, been one of the great fruits of the Council, a Church engaged as never before at all levels in talking and praying about what it means to be a Catholic in the modern world. But others feel only pain at the divisions that have opened up and fear that, in the rush to modernize, something essential may have been lost.

The Second Vatican Council

When Angelo Roncalli, the third of 13 children of peasant farmers from Bergamo, east of Milan, was elected as Pope John XXIII in 1958, he was regarded as a compromise candidate between those who wanted to continue Pius XII's legacy of standing resolutely apart from the modern world and those who wanted change and engagement. Pope John was also seen, at the age of 76, as a 'caretaker pope', someone whose reign would be brief and who would pave the way for a younger successor.

Catholicism believes that, when the cardinals of the Church gather to elect a new pope, they are guided by the Holy Spirit. It is how the Church explains some of the more unusual choices made in the line that is the Apostolic Succession. Certainly, few expected that John XXIII, who had been a scholarly, popular but uncontroversial Patriarch (or Archbishop) of Venice before his election, would begin a Catholic revolution.

In person, he could not have been more different from the austere, unsmiling, careful Pius. John XXIII dispensed with protocol and mixed easily with the people of Rome, on visits to hospitals, churches and prisons and even on walkabouts in the streets. Romans quickly took him to their hearts as 'good Pope John', as did others.

> *'This was the secret of his personality. He loved people more than power.'*
> Cardinal Yves Congar, theologian and Council Father on John XXIII

He welcomed the leaders of other Christian Churches to Rome as 'brothers' – including, in 1960, Dr Geoffrey Fisher, the Archbishop of Canterbury, the first Anglican leader to meet a pope since the Reformation. John abandoned Catholicism's instinctive hostility to communism, instead seeking ways of opening a dialogue with governments behind the Iron Curtain, in a policy known as *Ostpolitik*.

In January 1959 he surprised everyone by announcing plans to call what is now known to history as the Second Vatican Council, a gathering of the world's 3,000 Catholic bishops in Rome, which would, as he put it, 'promote the unity of all Christian peoples'. It would, he said, 'restore the simple and pure lines which the face of Jesus Christ's Church wore at its birth'. It would furthermore be an opportunity for *aggiornamento* – literally a 'bringing up to date' of Catholicism with the modern world.

The Council opened on 11 October 1962 and lasted for four sessions, taking place in consecutive autumns through to 1965. It was enthusiastically reported to the world by the Church and secular press and by the international media, enthralled by the sight of such an unchanging institution as the Catholic Church gathering to reform itself.

Those in the Curia who regarded John's initiative with suspicion hoped to restrict the Council Fathers' remit, but the Pope did away with such caution when he told the assembled prelates, in his opening address, to fashion a new pastoral – or practical – approach rather than engage in sterile academic debate. Ten commissions were given the task of drafting documents in areas such as theology, liturgy and mission. These documents would then be debated by the whole Council, amended and finally approved. John moved decisively early on to remove obstacles to free discussion and gave his support to the bishops when they rejected the narrow guidelines laid down for draft documents by the Curia. A revolution was well under way by the time of John's death in June 1963. His successor, Paul VI (1963–78), enthusiastically continued his predecessor's work.

THE KEY CHANGES

1 *Lumen Gentium* – The Dogmatic Constitution on the Church (November 1964) – reiterates traditional teaching that 'the sole Church of Christ which in the Creed we profess to be One, Holy, Catholic and Apostolic' is 'the Catholic Church, which is governed by the successor of Peter and by the bishops in communion with him', but adds: 'Nevertheless, many elements of sanctification and of truth are found outside its visible confines.' One result is that, when Anglicans convert to Catholicism today, they do not have to be baptised, since the Catholic Church recognizes their Anglican baptism as valid. They are simply received into the Church.

2 *Lumen Gentium* also tackles how the Catholic Church sees itself and rejects the hierarchical model – with clergy making the rules and laity obeying them – in favour of a vision of the whole Church as 'the people of God'. It stresses the equality of vocation to the clerical and lay life, to priesthood and marriage, and sets out the principal role of those in high office in the Church as being to serve fellow Catholics and the world.

3 *Unitatis Redintegratio* – The Decree of Ecumenism (November 1964) – sees the Council Fathers endorsing Pope John's support for the ecumenical movement, from which

Catholicism had previously stood apart. No longer was the goal to 'reconvert' Protestants to Catholicism, but rather the long-term aim became reunion of all separated brother and sister Churches, to be achieved through dialogue and common prayer.

4 *Nostra Aetate* – The Declaration on the Relationship of the Church with Non-Christian Religions (October 1965) – stresses Catholicism's sincere reverence for other faiths such as Hinduism and Buddhism, its common ground with Islam, and its rejection of the accusation that the Jewish people can be blamed for the death of Jesus.

5 *Sacrosanctum Concilium* – The Constitution on the Sacred Liturgy (December 1963) – promotes the 'active participation' of the laity in the liturgy and concedes that parts of the Mass could henceforth be celebrated in the vernacular – that is, in the local language – rather than Latin, as before.

6 In *Dei Verbum* – the Dogmatic Constitution on Divine Revelation (November 1965) – the Council Fathers encourage a much greater role for scripture in the life of the Church, advocate the wider availability of the Bible in the 'mother tongues' of the faithful, and instruct both clergy and laity to undertake Bible study.

7 In *Christus Dominus* – The Decree on the Pastoral Office of Bishops in the Church (October 1965) – the Council holds up the example of the Apostles working with their leader, Saint Peter, and orders that in all countries there should be a local bishops' conference able to make decisions on the application of the general teaching of Catholicism in the context of their area. It promotes more international synods – or gatherings of bishops – as a way of encouraging greater co-operation throughout the global Catholic Church.

8 *Gaudium et Spes* – The Pastoral Constitution on the Church in the Modern World (December 1965) – embodies, in the spirit of the whole Council, a desire to engage in a dialogue with the secular world.

Aftermath of the Council

'During the Second Vatican Council, the Catholic Church enjoyed a generally high public standing. At the beginning of the third millennium after Christ, however, it is being attacked more than ever in some quarters.'

Theologian and priest Hans Kung in *The Catholic Church: A Short History* (2001)

The engagement with the world sought by the Council Fathers was given dramatic expression when Pope Paul VI began travelling to meet his global flock. For over 100 years, popes had rarely strayed outside Rome and the Vatican. In 1964 Paul journeyed to Bombay to attend the Eucharistic Congress there, and in 1965 addressed the United Nations General Assembly to urge peace. He also renewed Catholicism's central administration, the Curia, in an effort to make it more outward-looking. In 1967 he established the Vatican's own Commission for Justice and Peace.

Key idea

Pope Paul VI was the first pontiff in modern times to go to visit his flock rather than wait for them to come to him.

Such was the pace of change generated by the Second Vatican Council that many Catholics were not content, however, with the speed of the implementation of its various pronouncements. They believed that the spirit of the Council demanded that the overhaul of familiar teachings had to continue further, into areas not dealt with by the Council Fathers.

Others, from the opposite end of the spectrum of Catholic views, were pressing Paul to use his authority to block some of the reforms proposed by the Council. Prominent among them was Archbishop Marcel Lefebvre (1905–91), a French Holy Ghost Father who had worked for most of his life in Senegal and West Africa. He engaged popular sympathy among some Catholics by his outspoken demand that the Mass must remain in Latin and that the rite of the Council of Trent, rather than the updated, vernacular forms of the New Rite, introduced from 1970 , continue to be used.

For many Catholics this change to the liturgy was the most contentious of the fruits of the Council. The distinguished Catholic historian Christopher Dawson (1889–1970) summed up their distress when he wrote in opposition to what was called the Vernacular Movement:

> The existence of a common liturgical language of some kind is a sign of the Church's mission... to create a bond of unity between the peoples. The nations that are still divided from one another by the barriers of race and language leave their divisions and antipathies at the door of the Church and worship together in a tongue which belongs to none and yet which is common to all.

However, Lefebvre's own rebellion went deeper. He rejected wholesale almost every aspect of the Council's work. For many years, the Vatican tried to reach some sort of accommodation with him and his small but dedicated band of followers, but when he began ordaining bishops who shared his views and, he intended, would continue his work after his death, he was excommunicated in 1988. He died in 1991, but in recent years there have been renewed efforts in the Vatican at reconciliation with those who followed him into schism.

CONFUSION AND CONFLICT
The majority of Catholics, however, were simply confused by what the changes would mean for their everyday lives and worship. Their parish churches, for instance, had to be reordered to accommodate the new-style liturgy, with the priest no longer standing at the altar with his back to the congregation. Priest and congregation were henceforth to participate together in the feast. So the altar rails, which had previously cordoned off the altar from the pews, were removed. And during Mass everyone was now expected to mingle and offer each other the 'Sign of Peace'.

Out, too, went time-honoured ceremonies and rites, while rephrasing ancient Latin into the vernacular allowed many people to engage and participate more fully in the Catholic liturgy. However, some felt that something of its mystery and drama had been lost in translation.

The changes in the liturgy encouraged hopes of still more change and reform. Two issues in particular dominated the decade after the Council. The first was the question of birth control. During the Council's debate on what was to become *Gaudium et Spes*, several of the bishops had urged the Catholic Church, as part of its engagement with the world, to re-examine its attitude to birth control. Catholic teaching was that only the so-called 'rhythm method' – abstinence during periods when conception was likely – was permissible, but it had a high failure rate, condemned Catholic couples to long periods without sexual relations, and moreover seemed to reinforce the idea that sex's primary purpose was procreation. With the liberation in attitudes to sex sweeping across Europe and the developed world in the 1960s, Catholicism was once again, its critics said, preaching ideals that were out of step with the reality of people's lives.

Part of that 1960s sexual revolution was the wide availability of the generally reliable oral contraceptive pill. It allowed women to take control of their own fertility for the first time. One of its inventors was an American Catholic obstetrician and gynaecologist, John Rock (1890–1984). He argued passionately in Church circles that it was a moral way of limiting the number of children a couple could produce.

Pope Paul referred the whole matter to a 64-strong commission of doctors, sociologists, population experts and theologians. It came back to him with two reports. The majority was in favour of reform. The minority – including some senior cardinals – opposed change. After much hesitation, Paul VI sided with the minority.

In July 1968 Paul VI published *Humanae Vitae* – 'On Human Life'. His insistence that sex was something for heterosexual couples within marriage came as no surprise, but his demand that 'every marriage act must remain open to life' disappointed many Catholics who had already, in their own bedrooms, anticipated a change of heart and started to use contraception.

Case study: Contraception

The Catholic Church does not object per se to a couple wishing to limit the number of children they have, but it insists that this can be done only by so-called 'natural' methods of contraception. These mostly involve abstinence from sex during the woman's fertile period.

One of the most popular of these Church-approved methods is the Billings Method, devised by two Australian Catholic doctors, John Billings and his wife, Evelyn Billings. They had nine children. Though it is often referred to by critics as 'Vatican Roulette' on account of its allegedly poor success rate, the World Health Organization has rated it at 98.5-per-cent successful in avoiding pregnancy.

The Billings Method is based on observing and recording the changing, developing pattern of cervical mucus secretion and sensation at the vulva. Its supporters point out that it teaches women to understand their own bodies and puts control of their fertility in their hands. Furthermore, they add, it does not require them to become dependent on often expensive pharmaceutical means of contraception. The Vatican alleges that the Billings Method is unfairly attacked by those who have an interest in the pharmaceutical industry making profits from the administration of chemical contraception.

The method is most effective when women can attend classes to learn how to monitor the rhythms of their bodies. It therefore requires time and commitment, as well as the support of both partners in a couple. Opponents suggest that it is therefore ill suited to the lives of the very poorest women, who face a daily struggle to eat and stay alive, and don't necessarily have the time to monitor and record their monthly cycles.

AN EXODUS OF PRIESTS

Linked with the dismay caused by *Humanae Vitae* and the Church's refusal to go with the times on the matter of contraception was a second, broader issue. Swept up in the heady atmosphere of the aftermath of the Council and its challenging decrees and constitutions, many priests and religious people began to question and experiment in their ministry, claiming to be following the spirit of Vatican II. They took at face value the words in *Lumen Gentium* that 'the body of the faithful as a whole, anointed as they are by the Holy One, cannot err in matters of belief'.

This inevitably brought them into conflict with their local bishops. *Lumen Gentium* had also expressed the view that the Catholic Church must remain a hierarchical organization. In the ensuing battles, many priests and nuns ended up leaving the active ministry. A significant number of them married, no longer able to justify the demand that they remain celibate. Yet most also remained as devout and practising Catholics, part of the priesthood of the laity.

Key idea

The Second Vatican Council and its aftermath saw a large number of priests and nuns abandon their ministry in frustration at the slow pace of reform.

The disappointment caused by *Humanae Vitae* only increased this exodus. Some estimates put the number of priests worldwide who left the active ministry at 100,000. *Humanae Vitae*, moreover, caused a wider crisis of authority in Catholicism. In his novel *How Far Can You Go?*, the British writer David Lodge, at the time a practising Catholic with a young family, summed up the impact of *Humanae Vitae* on his and many others' faith:

> If a Catholic couple decided, privately and with a conscience, to use contraceptives, there was nothing that priest, bishop or pope could do to stop them… Thus contraception was the issue on which many lay Catholics first attained moral autonomy, rid themselves of superstition, and ceased to

regard their religion as, in the moral sphere, an encyclopaedic rulebook in which a clear answer was to be found to every possible question of conduct.

Until the Second Vatican Council, Catholics had, in public at least, felt bound in most circumstances by the decisions handed down by the papacy. The Council inspired them to trust in their own moral judgements. Now, over possibly the most intimate and important decision they could make – how many children to have – *Humanae Vitae* seemed to force them to conclude that all the Council's talk of clergy and laity acting as one counted for nothing. Here was the Church reverting to type and imposing its wishes – in this case, an all-male hierarchy insisting on its right to regulate a woman's fertility.

Yet it had no effective sanction. No one could punish Catholic couples for having fewer children. No one but the couple could know what went on in their bedroom. Even if the use of the Pill or condoms was admitted in the confessional, most priests would grant absolution and the couple could carry on as before. It was a watershed in the moral authority of the papacy and the *magisterium* of the Church.

Key idea

The decision by many Catholics to make up their own minds over contraception, in defiance of the Vatican, had a knock-on effect in terms of their willingness to follow to the letter other aspects of Catholic teaching.

John Paul II

The last years of Paul VI's papacy saw a draining away of the enthusiasm unleashed by the Council, both in the Pope himself and within Catholicism. In its place came confusion as to what it meant to be a Catholic. Paul himself retreated ever more into the Vatican and died there, after a long illness. He was followed briefly by John Paul I (26 August–28 September 1978). This was Albino Luciani, another former Patriarch of Venice, who died after just 33 days in office. Rumours that he had been murdered were later conclusively refuted.

At the second conclave in a year, the cardinals unexpectedly chose Karol Józef Wojtyła, the Cardinal Archbishop of Kraków in Poland, to become Pope John Paul II. As a young bishop, he had participated in the Second Vatican Council and, it was hoped, would be able to sort out its legacy.

A papacy of firsts

Pope John Paul II (1978–2005) was:

▶ the first non-Italian to lead the Catholic Church for 455 years
▶ the first Slav to sit on the throne of Saint Peter
▶ the youngest holder of the office, at 58, for 130 years
▶ the first pontiff to travel the globe
▶ the first pope since the Reformation to visit Britain
▶ the first bishop of Rome since Saint Peter to visit the Rome synagogue
▶ the creator of more new saints in 27 years than his predecessors in the previous 500
▶ the author of more encyclicals and letters than any recent pope.

John Paul II's attitude to the fundamental changes within Catholicism that followed the Second Vatican Council was a complicated one. There were regular suggestions that he wished to 'put the clock back', especially when in 1985 he called a Special Synod of the world's bishops to examine the Council's legacy – 20 years after it had closed. But such criticisms were essentially misplaced. His true mission seems to have been to reflect and reach clarity on some of the matters that had become contentious and divisive in the rush to implement the Council's teachings.

John Paul epitomized both the socially radical aspect of Catholicism, which puts a premium on the fight for social justice, and its traditional, unchanging stance in the face of a secular world where scientific developments are now transforming the way people live at ever-greater speed. So he was simultaneously a champion of the developing world, calling repeatedly for the cancellation of Third World debt, and an implacable opponent of demands to approve new developments in the field of human fertilization and embryology.

He also spoke out loudly and clearly in defence of a traditional Catholic code of sexual ethics that made no concessions to the late twentieth century. John Paul in one sense simply endorsed everything that Paul VI had said on the question, but he sharpened it to an extraordinary degree, refusing to give any ground to those Catholics who had ignored *Humanae Vitae*'s teachings. Catholics who practised artificial birth control, he said in 1984, were 'denying the sovereignty of God', thus becoming, in effect, atheists.

ECUMENISM
While respectful of other religious traditions, and personally warm in his relationship with the leaders of other Churches, John Paul II would not countenance making the core compromises in Catholic doctrine that would be necessary to change the inter-church movement into something more than friendly exchanges of views.

Some of the ecumenical initiatives begun in the wake of the Council – and initially boosted by, for example, John Paul's visit in 1982 to Canterbury Cathedral, the seat of international Anglicanism – ground to a halt during his papacy over issues like ministry, Eucharist and authority. Catholicism still retains among its beliefs the 1896 encyclical *Apostolicae Curae*, in which the Anglican priesthood is declared to be 'absolutely null and utterly void'. John Paul refused all urgings to rescind this document.

In the spirit of engaging with the modern world, John Paul made a hallmark of his travelling. He was seen in the flesh by more people than any other pope in history. Even when ill health took its toll in his later years, brought on by Parkinson's disease (a diagnosis never formally confirmed by his doctors on account of the extreme secrecy that traditionally surrounds the health of the Pope in Catholicism), John Paul continued to visit his far-flung flock. His aim in undertaking such a demanding itinerary was threefold:

1 To offer himself as a visible sign of the unity of the worldwide Catholic Church

2 To stake an unmistakable claim for the papacy to a place on the stage of world political dramas

3 To hammer home, in his homilies when on tour, a basic set of beliefs around which all Catholics could rally. Top of the list were opposition to artificial contraceptives, abortion and divorce.

He was successful in drawing crowds and in inspiring great love and admiration in his flock, but there is little evidence that, on the three issues he chose to emphasize above all others, he made significant inroads into changing behaviour and secular norms. So, for example, he attracted widespread admiration among young people, who travelled in their hundreds of thousands, if not millions, to attend his special Youth Services and Days of Prayer, but there is little evidence that they then heeded his advice to wait until marriage to have sex and never to use condoms.

Spotlight

I was privileged to meet Pope John Paul in 1988, when accompanying a group of pilgrims with disabilities to Rome. His personal charm and charisma were immense. Every minute of our brief meeting remains vivid in my memory.

THE COLLAPSE OF COMMUNISM

John Paul's role in supporting and inspiring – and indeed funding via the Vatican – the free trade union movement Solidarity in his native Poland was undoubtedly his most obvious legacy. On his first visit home as Pope, in June 1979, he stood before one million Poles in Victory Square, Warsaw, where a 18-m (60-ft) high cross had been specially erected. No communist country had seen anything like it before. Here was the modern papacy intervening in the politics of the modern world to champion the aspirations of a people forced to live under communism for 40 years.

He became, according to many seasoned observers, the spark from heaven that set off the revolutions that tore down the Iron Curtain, first in Poland and then throughout Eastern Europe. And in keeping with his rejection of war as a legitimate means to settle humankind's disagreements, it was all largely done without violence – history's first great 'spiritual revolution'. The Kremlin grew to fear and loathe him so much, the Soviet leader Mikhail Gorbachev later tacitly admitted, that the KGB had some involvement in the 1981 assassination attempt on John Paul's life in St Peter's Square.

Key idea

John Paul II played a leading role in the collapse of communism in Eastern Europe.

John Paul's slow, drawn-out death, during which he never hid from his flock and the cameras as his once-athletic body was ravaged by Parkinson's disease, showed his profound courage and a strong sense of divinely ordained mission. However, by 2005, at the end of one of the longest pontificates in history, there were many Catholics – including senior cardinals – urging a change of direction from his successor.

Benedict XVI

The cardinals elected Benedict XVI, John Paul's former trusted senior advisor. As Prefect (or head) of the Congregation for the Doctrine of the Faith, the German Benedict (then Cardinal Joseph Ratzinger) had been responsible for ensuring theological orthodoxy and silencing dissenters in the Catholic Church. He also enjoyed a reputation as being hardline on many moral questions. In July 2003, for instance, he had labelled state recognition of homosexual partnerships as 'the legislation of evil'.

If he was chosen as the 'continuity' candidate, as Pope, Benedict surprised. His strongest urge was to shepherd all members of his sometimes fractured flock into a single corral. So his principal message was one of reconciliation. Soon after he took office, for example, he lunched with the radical Swiss theologian Father Hans Kung. Under John Paul II, Kung had been stripped of his licence to teach in Catholic universities, but here he was being invited back into the fold. And in his first encyclical, *Deus Caritas Est* ('God is Love'), published in December 2005, Benedict reflected on the importance of love in a poetic, positive and inclusive document.

Like John Paul, Benedict had also been present at the Second Vatican Council, when he was a young priest, as *peritus* (expert advisor) to Cardinal Joseph Frings of Cologne, one of the most outspoken reformers at the gathering. The Council clearly made an impact on him and on his pontificate.

Dig deeper

John Allen, *Cardinal Ratzinger* (Continuum, 2000).

Thomas Cahill, *Pope John XXIII* (Weidenfeld & Nicolson, 2002).

John Cornwell, *A Thief in the Night: The Death of Pope John Paul I* (Viking, 1989).

David Rice, *Shattered Vows: Exodus from the Priesthood* (Michael Joseph, 1990).

Edward Stourton, *John Paul II: Man of History* (Hodder, 2006).

For discussion and documents about the Second Vatican Council, go to the Vatican II – Voice of the Church website (http://www.vatican2voice.org)

Fact-check

1 When John XXIII was first elected, what was he seen as?
  a A caretaker pope
  b A reforming pope
  c A conservative pope
  d A new broom to sweep the Vatican clean

2 What is *Ostpolik*?
  a A Polish wine used in the consecration
  b The security force that protected John Paul II on his visits home to Poland
  c The Vatican's policy of engagement with communist governments
  d The drive to build more churches in Eastern Europe

3 How many bishops gathered in Rome for the Second Vatican Council?
  a 1,000
  b 2,000
  c 2,500
  d 3,000

4 Which future pope was a *peritus*, or expert advisor, at the Second Vatican Council?
  a Benedict XVI
  b John Paul I
  c John Paul II
  d Francis

5 What was the biggest changes Catholics saw in their parish church as a result of the Second Vatican Council?
  a It was painted a different colour
  b The Mass was in the local language rather than Latin
  c It was closed on a Sunday
  d Services were shared with other denominations

6 In which year did Pope Paul VI establish the Vatican's Justice and Peace Commission?
  a 1965
  b 1966
  c 1967
  d 1968

7 Which methods of birth control does the Catholic Church permit?
  a Condoms
  b The Pill
  c None
  d Natural ones

8 How many days did the pontificate of John Paul I last?
  a 30
  b 33
  c 65
  d 102

9 How many years separate John Paul II and the previous non-Italian pope?
  a 235
  b 287
  c 365
  d 455

10 Where had John Paul II been archbishop before his election as Pope?
  a Warsaw
  b Kraków
  c Gdansk
  d Jasna Góra

Catholicism under Pope Francis

In this chapter you will learn:

▶ *how papal election methods have changed*
▶ *when popes can abdicate*
▶ *what a cardinal is.*

Given how central the papacy is to Catholicism's distinctive identity and day-to-day operation, the method by which new popes emerge is of crucial importance. Saint Peter is said, in Catholic tradition, to have gathered an assembly of 24 priests and deacons and charged them with choosing his successor. The present method of election – by the College of Cardinals – is loosely modelled on this. In between times, however, a variety of other alternatives has been tried. It was only in the mid-twelfth century that Catholicism definitively restricted the vote to its principal clerics. In recent times there has been much talk of reforming the system, even involving the laity, but such changes as have been made have concerned small details.

'Eligio in Summum Pontificem' [I elect as Supreme Pontiff]
The wording on the ballot slips used now by cardinals to vote for the next pope

How popes used to be elected

During the first millennium of Catholicism, new popes emerged in a variety of ways:

- ▶ by election by assemblies of the clergy and people of Rome

- ▶ by popular acclamation at the funerals of their predecessors

- ▶ from among the small circle of deacons who had served the previous pope

- ▶ by being imposed by local noble families in Rome

- ▶ on the orders of kings, emperors and princes who regarded the papacy as in their gift.

At a synod in the Lateran in 1059, however, Pope Nicholas II (1058–61) took the first steps towards the system that exists today. Henceforth the electors would be the seven cardinal bishops of Rome, he decreed, with the city's cardinal deacons and then the people and ordinary clergy included only in the final stage to give their assent.

The reform remained contested for the next 100 years, not least by European monarchs who felt strongly that their views should be given precedence. And putative popes would still spend great sums on gifts for the Roman populace, to win their assent. In the mid-twelfth century, however, the right of cardinals to be the sole electors was finally established by the Church. A two-thirds majority was required from 1179 onwards.

Who becomes a cardinal?

The word 'cardinal' is thought to derive from the Latin for a hinge or a joint. It was a title first given to priests around the ninth century, and was linked closely with the five great basilicas of Rome. One theory is that the word was chosen because these 'cardinals' were seen as hinges or intermediaries between the papacy, which controlled the five basilicas (St John Lateran, St Peter's, St Lawrence outside the Walls, St Mary Major and St Paul outside the Walls), and the people of Rome.

The title had lost much of its original meaning by the time the cardinals were given control, in the eleventh century, over the election of the Pope, and later over the Church, in the inter-regnum between the death of one pope and the election of his successor. Yet a vestige of it remains to this day, with all cardinals of the Catholic Church having a 'titular parish church' in Rome under their protection.

The cardinals were described by Peter Damian (1007–72), the monastic leader and Church reformer, as 'the spiritual senators of the Roman Church' and they took on a relationship in regard to the papacy that had once been enjoyed by the great patriarchs of Constantinople, Jerusalem, Alexandria and Antioch, as key counsellors with a degree of independence, able in theory to rein in the papacy. They became effectively the senior management team of the Church, meeting with the Pope and each other, hearing legal cases and debating doctrine.

The term 'Curia', or 'court', used to describe cardinals and their assistants engaged in Rome in the Church bureaucracy, was first introduced by Urban II (1088–99) as he sought to reform the papal household. The cardinals' management of the

Church's finances, in particular, was later to be one of the major grievances of the Protestant reformers. At the time of the death of Leo X in 1521, when Martin Luther was facing the Diet of Worms, it was said that there were more than 2,150 posts in the Curia that could be bought, up to and including the role of the cardinal who was papal chamberlain.

From the twelfth century onwards, there were cardinals based in European cities other than Rome. Some of them – like Nicholas Breakspear, the future Hadrian IV (1154–9), the only English pope – served as legates, travelling to encourage Catholicism around Europe and impose the Pope's wishes. Others, like Cardinals Wolsey and Pole in sixteenth-century England, and Richelieu and Mazarin in seventeenth-century France, were powerful government ministers.

The cardinals' collective strength in the decision-making of the Church has always depended on their relationship with the reigning pope. If he is strong, they are usually weak, and vice versa. Popes have unfettered power to name cardinals, but the men they choose do not always do as their patron would wish.

Since 1630, cardinals of the Catholic Church have been given the title 'Eminence'. By tradition they wear scarlet. When they are chosen, it is often said that they have been 'given a red hat' by the Pope, though the colour is seen on them more often in the form of a scarlet skullcap, scarlet piping on their black cassocks, a scarlet belt (or *fascia*) and a scarlet cape (*ferraiolo*). Each cardinal is given a gold ring by the pontiff, to symbolize their bond.

Key idea

Cardinals are the most senior leaders in the Catholic Church. Few in number, they are easy to spot because they wear scarlet.

Papal conclaves

After a three-year hiatus from 1268 to 1271 when choosing a successor to Clement IV, new rules were introduced. The cardinal electors were to be held *cum clave* – locked in, 'with key' – until they could reach a decision. Locking the door was designed to focus their minds. It was even suggested that, if they took more than three days, their food should be rationed, but this was not adopted. The idea of the conclave was, however, established.

At 30, numbers of cardinal electors were small throughout the medieval and Renaissance periods. To counter a subsequent growth, Pope Sixtus V (1585–90) introduced a limit of 70. This remained in place until the times of John XXIII and the Second Vatican Council, when John sought to include a greater variety of voices in future conclaves. He did, however, enter new restrictions. He barred laymen, who had previously been able, in rare cases, to be cardinals. All holders of a red hat must now be clergy.

Paul VI was reported to be considering a reform of the electoral process to reflect the spirit of the Council – possibly giving a greater role to the heads of local bishops' conferences – but the only change he actually delivered was to exclude from voting those cardinals who had reached the age of 80. Pope John Paul II made further minor changes in 1996, on the occasion of the opening of a new accommodation block to house the cardinals during their deliberations.

Spotlight

St Martha's Hostel, the accommodation block opened in 1996, has since the election of Pope Francis become the papal residence. He uses the grand papal apartments on the third floor of the Apostolic Palace in the Vatican as his office, but lives in a simple, single room in this hostel for clerics, in line with his personal commitment to living a simple life. He takes his meals at the communal table with other priests staying there, telling an Italian magazine: 'I must live my life with others.'

How popes are elected now

Those cardinals aged under 80 on the day of the previous pope's death gather in the Sistine Chapel shortly after his funeral.

They are sworn to secrecy over their deliberations, on pain of excommunication. They cast a series of secret ballots, two each morning and two each afternoon. Potential candidates are identified as 'papabile' – capable of being Pope. If no verdict has been reached before nightfall, the cardinals go to the new Saint Martha's Hostel, alongside the Sistine Chapel, to sleep, and then start again the next day. (During conclaves in the past, they had been put up in a variety of small side rooms and broom cupboards around the chapel. It was feared that the new, more spacious quarters would increase the length of their deliberations but, with the rapid election of Benedict XVI in 2005, and Francis in 2013, it seemed that, if anything, they have had the opposite effect.)

Cardinals cast their votes on ballot papers that are then placed in a chalice on the altar underneath Michelangelo's *Last Judgement*. Catholicism believes that the cardinals will be guided in making their choices not only by their assessment of the needs of the Church but also by the Holy Spirit.

To be elected, a candidate requires a two-thirds majority. In 1996, however, Pope John Paul II changed the rules so that if, after an agreed period of time, the cardinals so wish it, they can opt for a simple absolute majority of 50 per cent plus one.

If the ballot has proved inconclusive, the ballot papers are threaded together and burnt, producing a grey smoke that can be seen rising out of a chimney on the roof of the Sistine Chapel. Once a verdict has been reached, however, a chemical (it used to be wet straw) is added as the ballot papers are put in the flames, in order to turn the smoke white and so alert the world to the election of a new pope. Since 2005 it has also been decreed that the bells of St Peter's will ring, to clear up any debate in the square outside about what colour the smoke is.

Once chosen, the successful candidate puts on the white cassock of the Pope (three are set aside before the conclave, in small, medium and large sizes, to cover all eventualities) and is led to the papal balcony, high above St Peter's Square, by the Dean of the College of Cardinals. The Dean emerges on to the balcony and declares to the waiting crowd, *'Habemus papam'* – 'We have a pope.'

In the past 200 years, no conclave has lasted more than five days. Throughout the history of the papacy, 79 per cent of popes chosen have been Italians, 38 per cent Romans. In the nineteenth century all popes came from the Papal States. However, with the election of, first, a Pole at the end of the twentieth century, a German in 2005, and then an Argentinian in 2013 – 'from the end of the world' is how Pope Francis described himself – there is believed to be no obstacle now within Catholicism to a pope from anywhere around the globe. With a larger than ever proportion of the cardinal electors coming from the developing world, it is thought it will be only a matter of time before one of their number becomes Pope and a symbol of a truly universal Church.

Those considered contenders for the papacy are referred to as 'papabile'. The papacy is a post that one must accept reluctantly. Any show of wanting it, or worse, campaigning for it, would be taken amiss. Hotly tipped front-runners, it is held, rarely emerge victorious as Pope. That said, the then Cardinal Ratzinger's address at John Paul II's funeral in 2005, and his words as the cardinals gathered to go into conclave, are reported to have made a profound impact.

Case study: The election of Pope Francis

Though cardinal-voters are sworn to secrecy over what actually happens in a conclave, there have been sufficient leaks from the gathering in 2013 to produce a strong outline of how the unfancied Argentinian Cardinal Jorge Mario Bergoglio came to be elected as Pope Francis. In the 2005 conclave that followed the death of John Paul II, Bergoglio had surprised many by being the leading 'reformist' candidate. He came second in the fourth and final ballot to the 'continuity' candidate, Cardinal Joseph Ratzinger, who took the name Benedict XVI.

But by 2013 there were other more prominent Latin American candidates and Bergoglio's name was hardly mentioned. Before the 115 voting cardinals went into the conclave on Tuesday 12 March, however, there was a series of more public meetings, called general congregations. The front-runner going into that process was Cardinal Angelo Scola of Milan, said to have Pope Benedict's blessing, but his speech did not, it was reported, impress, whereas a brief three-and-a-half-minute contribution from Bergoglio did.

'Put simply,' he told his fellow cardinal-electors, 'there are two images of Church: a Church which evangelizes and comes out of herself, [or] of a worldly Church living within herself, of herself, for herself.' His preference was for the first, and he caught the mood, with many wanting to see the power of the Vatican Curia reduced.

In the first ballot, Scola took the lead with – according to most leaked reports – 35 votes. Bergoglio had 20 and the Canadian Marc Ouellet, another Vatican 'insider', close to Benedict, received 15. In the second and third ballots, on the morning of Wednesday, 13 March, Bergoglio's numbers rose, as other minor candidates dropped out, while Scola's remained static. At lunch that day Ouellet is said to have indicated his support for Bergoglio, who took the lead in the fourth ballot that afternoon and was elected with 90 of the 115 votes in the final round of the day.

Can popes abdicate?

'In order to govern the bark of Saint Peter and proclaim the gospel, both strength of mind and body are necessary.'
Pope Benedict XVI, announcing his abdication on 11 February 2013

The papacy is traditionally a role in which the incumbent continues until he dies. During the long final illness of Pope John Paul II, as he struggled with the debilitating effects of Parkinson's disease, it was said that he did consider the question of abdication, but finally ruled it out, believing that, if God wished him to relinquish the post, he would hasten his death. His successor, Benedict XVI, however, took a different view, and after almost eight years in the job, as he approached his 86th birthday, he took the world by surprise and resigned, explaining that the challenges of the job were simply beyond him. He was the first pope to do so in 600 years.

Spotlight

John Paul II is reported to have rejected the idea of abdicating because he worried that, if retired, he would inevitably become a focus for those dissatisfied with his successor, and he believed that maintaining Church unity was more important than his own comfort. As Pope Emeritus, however, still living inside the Vatican, Benedict has been careful to keep out of the public eye and to maintain a strict public silence on the record of his successor.

Abdication is specifically allowed for in Canon Law. As long as the decision is 'made freely and properly manifested', it states, the abdication does not need to be 'accepted by anyone'. There are examples in the early Church of popes who abdicated, in circumstances that have been lost to history. Two later examples stand out: Pope Benedict IX (1033–44) abdicated in order to do penance as a monk for his sinful ways, but within two years he was trying forcibly to reclaim the papacy. And Pope Celestine V, elected in 1294 after two years' deadlock, was said to have been chosen on account of his blameless life as a monk-hermit. But that lifestyle left him ill equipped to deal with the demands made on a pope, as he realized quickly. He was also 85. So, six months later, he published a decree allowing papal abdication, which he then took advantage of.

Not all approved of his decision. His contemporary the great Italian poet Dante (1265–1321) placed Celestine in the first circle of Hell in his *Inferno*, for his 'great refusal'. Meanwhile Celestine's successor, fearful that he might become a rallying point for those disgruntled with the papacy, had him imprisoned until his death.

Key idea

Popes can abdicate but have rarely done so for fear of destabilizing the Church.

The Vatican

The central administration of the Catholic Church is known variously as the Curia, the Holy See and the Vatican. The last comes from the geographical area where it is located. The land to the west of the river Tiber, where the Vatican now stands, was an ancient pagan shrine that became, around the time of Jesus, a Roman pleasure garden. It was here that Saint Peter was executed in AD 64.

Spotlight

The word 'see' – as in Holy See – comes from the Latin for 'seat' and indicates the geographical base or seat of a bishop, that is, the headquarters of his diocese. Since early Church times, the bishopric of Rome has been called the 'Holy See'. Diplomats use this phrase rather than the Vatican City State, so they are 'ambassadors to the Holy See'.

When Christianity achieved official recognition in the Roman Empire in the fourth century, a basilica was built in memory of Saint Peter, and a century later a papal palace was added. In the ninth century Pope Leo IV (847–55) built walls around what became known as the 'Leonine City', to protect St Peter's from attack by Rome's opponents. He was prompted to act when raiders had emptied Saint Peter's tomb and scattered his bones.

However, until the fourteenth century popes did not reside in the Vatican. They lived at the Lateran Palace in the heart of the city of Rome, next to the basilica of St John Lateran, the mother church of Rome. On their return from exile in Avignon at the end of the fourteenth century, the Lateran Palace had fallen into disrepair and so popes made their home in either the Vatican or the Quirinale Palace.

When Italian forces took over Rome in 1870, the Quirinale was seized and would later become the official residence of the Italian president. Pope Pius IX retreated into the Vatican, vowing never to come out again until his sovereignty was restored. In 1929 the Italian government, under Benito Mussolini, resolved what had become an embarrassing impasse by coming to an agreement with Pope Pius XI (1922–39) which created the Vatican City State as a new sovereign country – that is, not a restoration of the Papal States – ruled over by the Bishop of Rome.

Key idea

Because of the Vatican City State, the Pope, uniquely among religious leaders, is both a head of state and the head of a church.

At 44 hectares (110 acres), the Vatican is the smallest sovereign state in the world and is largely enclosed by the Leonine Walls, and their subsequent extensions, and by the river Tiber. Several other sites on Italian territory were granted to the new state, including the papal summer palace outside Rome at Castel Gandolfo, and the other four great basilicas of the city. As well as a tiny railway station of its own, a heliport and a Post Office issuing its own stamps, the Vatican boasts its own radio station. Vatican Radio broadcasts to the world, putting across a distinctively Catholic message. The daily newspaper, *L'Osservatore Romano*, contains full details of all papal visits, meetings and pronouncements. The state also has its own police force in the colourfully dressed Swiss Guards. A force of Catholic Swiss troops has served popes since Julius II (1503–13). Their blue, red, orange and yellow ceremonial outfit is said to have been designed by Michelangelo, but there is no evidence for this.

> 'The curia is called upon to improve itself, always improve itself and grow in communion, holiness and knowledge to fully realize its mission. Like every body, like every human body, it is exposed to illnesses, malfunctioning, infirmity. They are illnesses and temptations that weaken our service to God.'
>
> Pope Francis, in his annual address to the Curia, December 2014

Most of the Vatican's territory, plus various outbuildings in Rome treated as Vatican sovereign territory, are used to house the Curia, the central bureaucracy of the Church, headed by senior churchmen but also employing significant numbers of laypeople (men and women) in the ranks. The principal departments of the Curia are:

- the Secretariat of State (effectively the Vatican's Foreign Ministry, dealing with other governments)

- the Congregation for the Doctrine of the Faith (once the Holy Office in charge of the Inquisition, now concerned with discipline and theological orthodoxy)

- the Congregation for the Causes of Saints (in charge of the process for making saints)

- the Congregation for Catholic Education (overseeing seminaries and Catholic educational institutions)

- the Congregation for Bishops (in charge of appointing and monitoring bishops).

There are also the various courts and tribunals of the Sacred Roman Rota which interpret questions of Canon Law; the Vatican Bank, officially known as the Institute for Works of Religion and a source of great scandal in the 1980s because of its links with disgraced financiers; the Vatican's celebrated museums; and its equally renowned library, including the Secret Archive. The resident population of the Vatican City State is around 800.

Spotlight

American Archbishop Paul Marcinkus, a former bodyguard to Pope Paul VI, was head of the Vatican Bank until 1990. His dealings with the disgraced Italian financier Roberto Calvi, found hanging from London's Blackfriars Bridge in 1982, propelled Marcinkus and the bank into the spotlight. Though the Vatican denied all liability for the collapse of Calvi's Banco Ambrosiano, it eventually agreed to pay creditors around £150 million.

Conclusion

No other leader of a world religion retains his own sovereign country. The existence of the Vatican City State gives the Catholic Church a place by right at many international gatherings and organizations. Because the Pope does not have to worry about the effect of his remarks, actions or teachings on any secular 'host government', he is in theory free to do and speak as he sees right. However, the reality is that the Vatican City State is entirely dependent on Italy to function – in terms of water, electricity, gas, transport and so on – and that relationship with Italy remains sensitive and sometimes fraught.

Dig deeper

Mary Hollingsworth, *Conclave* (Thistle, 2013).

Rupert Shortt, *Benedict XVI* (Hodder, 2005).

John Thavis, *The Vatican Diaries* (Penguin, 2013).

Paul Vallely, *Pope Francis: Untying the Knot* (Bloomsbury, 2013).

Fact-check

1 In which century was the term 'curia' first used to described papal servants?
- **a** First
- **b** Tenth
- **c** Eleventh
- **d** Twelfth

2 How should you address a cardinal?
- **a** Your Honour
- **b** Your Reverence
- **c** Your Majesty
- **d** Your Eminence

3 What colour in their attire signals a cardinal?
- **a** Scarlet
- **b** Mauve
- **c** Black
- **d** White

4 When were non-clerics banned from being appointed cardinals?
- **a** In the first century
- **b** In the sixth century
- **c** In the sixteenth century
- **d** In the twentieth century

5 Where does Pope Francis live?
- **a** In the Apostolic Palace in the Vatican
- **b** In the Quirinale Palace in Rome
- **c** In the St Martha's Hostel
- **d** Next to St John Lateran Basilica in Rome

6 Where do Catholic cardinals gather to vote for a new pope?
- **a** In the Sistine Chapel
- **b** At the main altar in St Peter's
- **c** By Saint Peter's grave
- **d** In St Peter's Square

7 Who is guiding cardinals when they place their votes?
   a Bookmakers
   b The Holy Spirit
   c Jesus
   d Catholic parishes

8 How do the cardinals first tell the outside world that they have chosen a new pope?
   a With a press release
   b By a puff of white smoke
   c By appearing on the papal balcony
   d By publishing the result of their ballot

9 Which force is responsible for guarding the Pope?
   a The Italian army
   b The United Nations
   c The Swiss Guards
   d The Vatican police

10 When do Catholic cardinals stop being able to vote for a new pope?
   a When they die
   b When they are 65
   c When they are 75
   d When they are 80

The Church on the ground

In this chapter you will learn:

▶ *why priests are different from laymen*
▶ *about the vocations crisis*
▶ *in what circumstances married men can be priests.*

For many Catholics, the Vatican can seem a very long way away – geographically and spiritually. Even with the unprecedented travelling regime undertaken by John Paul II – he visited 130 countries in all in his 27 years as Pope, with pictures of him kissing airport tarmac among the most familiar of his pontificate – and the more recent journeying around the globe of Pope Francis, the worldwide Catholic Church remains a far-flung body. John Paul and his successor, Benedict XVI, changed the composition of the College of Cardinals to bring more figures into its ranks from the developing world. Once again, Pope Francis is continuing that trend, even accelerating it, but the leadership and decision-making establishment of Catholicism is still disproportionately European and Italian in make-up.

For Catholics in the developing world, then, and indeed for many Catholics in the developed world, their routine interaction with the hierarchy of their Church is through the local bishop, and most of all through the local priest.

The episcopate

> 'He must not have been married more than once, and he must be temperate, discreet and courteous, hospitable and a good teacher.'
> Saint Paul in his First Letter to Timothy (3:2) on what makes a good local church leader

The word 'bishop' comes from the Greek *episkopos*, 'overseer', a term used in the New Testament. Sometimes, the word is translated as 'elder'. As the early Church developed, however, the term 'elder' dropped out of use and was replaced by 'bishop'. A bishop would often be the leader of the Christians in major towns or cities, a pattern maintained to this day. From the second century onwards, as set out in the writings of key figures such as Clement of Alexandria (150–211), the task of ordaining priests was reserved to bishops.

Where it is possible today, a bishop also bestows the sacrament of confirmation on one of his regular visits to the parishes of his diocese. It is also the role of the bishop, each Maundy Thursday (immediately before the Easter celebration), to anoint sacred oils at the Mass of chrism in the diocesan cathedral. This practice follows the traditions of anointing described in the Old Testament, as the sacred oils are then used by priests and the bishop in bestowing the sacraments of baptism, confirmation, holy orders and of the sick, as will be described in Chapter 10.

Throughout the history of Catholicism bishops have filled many high political offices, but the 1983 *Code of Canon Law* expressly forbids this. In the wake of the Second Vatican Council, all bishops were required to join together into national bishops' conferences. CELAM, the Latin American and Caribbean bishops' organization, is one of the largest examples of this in the world. It has its own secretariat. One of the bishops will be chosen as president, and others will take on specific responsibilities for areas of interest, such as liturgy, education, international development and so forth.

Spotlight

Pope John Paul II's opposition to priests holding political office caused the American Jesuit Father Robert Drinan to stand down in 1980 as the Democratic representative in Congress for Massachusetts. He had been elected in 1971 on an anti-Vietnam War ticket. More recently, both Cardinal Basil Hume and his successor as leader of the Catholic Church in England and Wales, Cardinal Cormac Murphy-O'Connor, declined invitations from politicians to be nominated for seats in the House of Lords, the upper chamber of the British Parliament, since it would constitute a political office.

Bishops are appointed by the Vatican's Congregation for Bishops, taking advice from the Papal Nuncio (or ambassador) resident in the country in question. When a vacancy arises, he will produce a *terna*, or list of three possible candidates, on the basis of his soundings with local Catholics and their leaders. The final decision belongs to Rome, which has the right to reject the *terna*, ask for another, or simply pick its own candidates. No interference from local political leaders is allowed. It is the insistence of the Chinese communist authorities on having a say in the choice of Catholic bishops that has caused it to clash repeatedly with the Vatican and for an 'underground' church to emerge there, loyal only to the Pope.

Key idea

In the modern Catholic Church, all bishops are appointed by the Vatican.

Bishops have to tender their resignation to the Pope at the age of 75, but in some circumstances are allowed to stay on longer. The colour worn by Catholic bishops is traditionally purple. Their garb includes a pointed hat (mitre), a shepherd's staff (crozier) and a pectoral cross, worn around their neck.

There are several types of bishops within Catholicism:

▶ **Archbishops** head major dioceses and act as 'metropolitans' or overseers of neighbouring dioceses.

▶ **Suffragan bishops**, or Ordinaries, are the heads of the individual dioceses that make up each metropolitan area or archdiocese.

▶ **Auxiliary bishops** are often appointed in large dioceses, to assist the bishop or archbishop, especially if he has other roles in the Church such as cardinal or member of a key Vatican commission.

▶ **Titular bishops** do not head real dioceses. Their title is derived from an ancient and now lost diocese of the Church. They will usually work in the Curia.

▶ **Coadjutor bishops** are appointed by the Vatican to assist the existing bishop in their diocese, especially if the latter is in ill health, and will succeed when the existing bishop stands down.

▶ **Bishops Emeritus** are retired bishops who often continue to serve in their diocese.

Spotlight

The Vatican's choice of bishops can be controversial. When Wolfgang Haas was appointed auxiliary bishop in the Swiss diocese of Chur in 1988, there were widespread local protests about his alleged ultra-traditionalist views. At his installation, several hundred demonstrators lay down to form a human carpet outside the cathedral's main doors. The Vatican refused to back down and in 1997 promoted him to be Archbishop of Vaduz in Liechtenstein.

The nature of priesthood

'Among all human affection, the human spirit is especially held fast by married love... consequently the marriage bond is to be avoided at all costs by those tending to perfection.'
Saint Thomas Aquinas (1225–74), 'On the Perfection of Spiritual Life'

To become a Catholic priest, you have to be male and willing to live a celibate life after ordination. For much of the twentieth century, a traditional regime existed whereby those wanting to be priests would, from the age of 11 or 12, enter a Junior Seminary and then move straight on to studies for the priesthood at the Major (adult) Seminary, often taken in conjunction with a degree.

However, in reaction to the large numbers who subsequently left the priesthood because they felt they had made a lifetime's commitment before they were mature enough to do so conclusively, it has become more usual now for candidates to join once they have left secondary school, and often university. Many seminaries, especially in the developed world, encourage those who feel they have a vocation to go and see something of life, before finally committing themselves.

Study for the priesthood is undertaken in a seminary, either in the local diocese, under the control of the local bishop, or elsewhere. Some candidates, especially those considered to have great academic potential, are sent to study in Rome. The basic training takes six years and includes time spent in parishes and learning by working alongside older priests. Many go on to take further qualifications, once a bishop has ordained them.

Today Catholicism talks of priesthood in relation to both the laity and the clergy. All are seen as having a vocation, because all are called to be Christians. So, in that sense, all believers are priests.

> 'There is a diversity of ministry [among Catholics] but a oneness of mission. Christ conferred on the Apostles and their successors the duty of teaching, sanctifying, and ruling in his name and power. But the laity likewise share in the priestly, prophetic, and royal office of Christ and therefore have their own share in the mission of the whole people of God in the Church and in the world.'
>
> *Apostolicam Actuositatem* – the Second Vatican Council's Decree on the Apostolate of the Laity, November 1965

But modern Catholicism also makes a crucial distinction. Some are called to be *ordained* priests. 'The ministerial priesthood differs in essence from the common priesthood of the faithful,' states the *Catechism of the Catholic Church*, 'because it confers a sacred power for the service of the faithful. The ordained ministers exercise their service for the People of God by teaching, divine worship and pastoral governance.'

This harks back to the spirit of what had been the practice of the Catholic Church up to then, namely placing priests on a higher level than the laity. Such a set-up was emphatically rejected at the Second Vatican Council and the two roles were seen as on a par, different but complementary.

In practice, however, many lay people continue to experience the Church as a hierarchical and clerical-dominated organization. For example, despite moves to encourage lay participation in the liturgy, many bishops in recent times have issued instructions curtailing what had been an expanding habit of having lay people preach at Mass. And Pope John Paul II was a firm believer in priests wearing their distinctive black cassock as they went about their daily life, rather than the same clothes as the laity.

The more profound question of priestly identity continues to concern the Church. To put it simply, is the priest just a social worker who says prayers? Catholicism responds that the priest is distinct from the layman in that he is both icon and leader of the community. The second description comes in part from the priest's role in the parish, and from the freedom to act in a leadership role that his celibate state should afford him by removing other commitments and demands on his time.

But it also draws on the first part of the answer – that he is an icon. Catholicism believes the priest stands in the place of Jesus, not just during the Mass when, at the consecration, he turns the bread and wine into the body and blood of Christ, as Jesus did at the Last Supper, but also in other aspects of his life and activities, particularly with regard to the Church's social mission. 'Through the ordained ministry, especially that of bishops and priests,' states the *Catechism of the Catholic Church*, 'the presence of Christ as head of the Church is made visible in the midst of the community of believers.'

Although Catholicism places the vocations of the laity and the priesthood on an equal footing, it discourages those who have been ordained from seeking to return to lay status. There is a bureaucratic process, administered by Rome and called laicization, but under Pope John Paul II it more or less ground to a halt. In the *Catechism of the Catholic Church*, it is written:

> It is true that someone validly ordained can, for grave reasons, be discharged from the obligations and functions linked to ordination, or can be forbidden to exercise them, but he cannot become a layman again in the strict sense, because the character imprinted by ordination is for ever. The vocation and mission received on the day of his ordination mark him permanently.

Key idea

Catholic priests must be male and celibate.

Celibacy

> 'There are eunuchs born that way from their mother's womb, there are eunuchs made so by men, and there are eunuchs who have made themselves that way for the sake of the kingdom of heaven. Let anyone accept this who can.'
>
> Jesus, speaking of celibacy in Matthew's gospel (19:10–12)

The priesthood of the Catholic Church is reserved to celibate males. Catholicism is the only one of the Christian Churches to insist upon this. Priests of the Orthodox tradition are permitted to marry, though only celibates fill the higher ranks of that Church. Martin Luther preached enthusiastically about the virtues of marriage for the clergy and followed his own advice by wedding a former nun, Katharina von Bora, who bore him six children.

For more than half of Catholicism's history, its priests were allowed to marry. Married men of proven virtue – *viri probati* – were prominent among the priests of the early Church. It was only in 1139, at the Second Lateran Council, that celibacy became mandatory. Some bishops did not enforce this ruling as forcefully as others and some married priests therefore continued into the sixteenth century, when they were finally outlawed by the Council of Trent.

Today, then, those who feel a vocation to the priesthood are also required to have a second vocation – to celibacy. There were several reasons why the Church changed its position:

1 The disreputable behaviour of some married priests who abandoned their wives, took lovers and tried to pass on Church property to their children.

2 The contrast between such behaviour and the example of the lives of celibate monks, living in communities dedicated to prayer and service, making real in their own lives the separation described by writers such as Thomas Aquinas between the spiritual and the physical.

3 The belief that a wife and children would inevitably distract a priest from his duties to his parishioners. Saint Paul wrote in his First Letter to the Corinthians (7:32), 'An unmarried man can devote himself to the Lord's affairs, all he need worry about is pleasing the Lord.'

4 The value placed on the celibate life as a 'sign of contradiction' in the secular world, a symbol of the rejection of that world's value system.

Most of these arguments relate to the practice of the Church, rather than directly to the scriptures. The celibacy rule is essentially based in the tradition of Catholicism. The one gospel passage quoted by those who support a celibate priesthood comes in Matthew 19, quoted above. Matthew's words were used by Pope John Paul II in his 1979 *Letter to the Priests of the World* as a justification for continuing the rule of celibacy.

Key idea

Catholicism is the only one of the Christian traditions to insist that its priests be both celibate and male.

The correct interpretation of that passage in Matthew's gospel (it is not included in the other three) has been widely debated by scholars. What Jesus is really condemning in the sections running up to it, some theologians point out, is men who commit adultery. Moreover, he seems to be responding to the suggestion from his disciples that, if you have to be faithful to just one woman, it is better not to marry at all, and therefore, by implication, to have several relationships. And it is important, the same theologians suggest, to note Jesus' final words: 'Let anyone accept this who can.' Even if the official interpretation of the passage is correct, it should not then be made into a blanket rule in favour of a celibate priesthood.

> 'Deprive the Church of honourable marriage and you will fill her with concubinage, incest and all manner of nameless vices.'
> Saint Bernard of Clairvaux in his *Sermons* (1135)

Catholicism argues that there is further justification for the rule of celibacy to be found in Saint Paul's First Letter to the Corinthians. 'Yes, it is a good thing for a man not to touch a woman,' he writes (7:1–2). However, he goes on: 'Yet to avoid immorality every man should have his own wife and every woman her own husband... otherwise Satan may take advantage of any lack of self-control to put you to the test' (7:5).

This cannot, therefore, be seen as a conclusive endorsement of priestly celibacy. Saint Paul does not appear to have found marriage attractive for himself. He regarded it as a distraction from preparing for the Second Coming of Christ. Yet, neither did he condemn it in others. 'To the unmarried and to widows, I say: it is good for them to stay as they are, like me. But if they cannot exercise self-control, let them marry, since it is better to be married than to be burnt up' (I Corinthians 7:8–9).

The Catholic Church, however, argues that the basis for priestly celibacy goes deeper than individual scriptural passages. It holds that the priest, at the altar, at the moment of consecration, stands in the place of Jesus at the Last Supper. And Jesus was, the gospels report, celibate and male. Hence the ordination of women cannot be considered.

While the celibacy rule is of relatively recent origin, the cult of virginity, in imitation of Christ, has been part of Catholicism from its earliest days. 'I consider there is nothing more calculated to cast a man's spirits down from the citadel', wrote Saint Augustine in the fifth century, 'than the blandishments of a woman.'

Today there are those who argue for a return to the earlier practice of married priests, on the practical grounds of tackling the shortage of vocations in Catholicism, particularly in the developed world and Latin America. While vocations continue to rise in Africa and Asia, they are at a low ebb in Europe and the Americas. Latin American bishops, for instance, report that congregations in remote areas may only see a Catholic priest once or twice a year because there are so few of them to go around.

Spotlight

The Second Vatican Council revived the ordained ministry of the permanent diaconate, part of the practice of the early Church. Permanent deacons can lead prayers, officiate at marriages, funerals and baptisms, and generally assist the priest in running a parish. They must be male, can be married (though must pledge not to remarry if their spouse dies) and are usually required to be of mature years. Worldwide numbers of deacons have grown significantly in recent years, from 29,000 in 2001 to 41,000 in 2011.

Numbers of priests

The 2013 *Annuario Pontificio* – the official yearbook of the Vatican – reports the following statistics regarding the priesthood:

	No. of priests worldwide	No. of seminarians worldwide
2011	413,418	120,616
2010	412,236	118,990

There are, however, wide regional variations. Numbers of priests have grown in the decade to 2011 in Africa (39.5 per cent) and in Asia (32 per cent), remained the same in the Americas, but fallen by 9 per cent in Europe. Over the same period, numbers of seminarians had increased by 30.9 per cent in Africa, 29.4 per cent in Asia, but fallen by 1.9 per cent in the Americas and 21.7 per cent in Europe.

Research carried out by the University of Fordham in 2002 reported the following statistics for Catholicism in the United States:

	No. of priests	No. of seminarians	No. of parishes without a resident priest
1930	27,000	16,300	0
1965	58,000	49,000	3 per cent
2002	45,000	4,700	15 per cent
2020*	31,000	N/A	25 per cent

* projected

Married priests

There is a small number of married priests in the Catholic Church. Officially, you can be both married and a priest if:

▶ you are a widower. It is not uncommon for a married man to choose to follow the path to ordination after the death of his wife.

▶ you are a married ex-Anglican priest. Under Pope John Paul II, a special dispensation was allowed for the ordination of married, convert Anglicans who had joined the Catholic

Church; and in 2009 Benedict XVI broadened this to offer Anglican dissenters their own 'ordinariate', or section in Catholicism, where they could continue with a married priesthood and the distinctive Anglican-Catholic liturgical practices.

▶ you are a member of one of the Eastern Rite Churches in communion with Rome.

To this official list might be added, unofficially, those men, ordained as Catholic priests, who have gone on to marry, but have not applied for, or been granted laicization, and who still regard themselves as priests.

Case study: Convert Anglican priest Father Peter Cornwell

Father Peter Cornwell was a senior Anglican priest in the university city of Oxford who converted to Catholicism in the 1985 and now serves as a Catholic priest. He was married to Hilary at the time of his conversion. 'My job now', he told me in an interview some years later, 'is to show that being a married priest works without bringing the skies down. Let's not treat a married priesthood as some great New Jerusalem. The Church has a very romantic notion of celibacy and a very romantic view of marriage. Neither will do.

'Reality is a much more sturdy base to build on, which is why I'm very hesitant about saying marriage is the answer to the problem [of a shortage of Catholic priests in the West]. I do know celibate priests who are so by vocation, and are totally reconciled. I'm hesitant, therefore, about setting up married priests as some kind of magic. That's not the case. What we do need are priests – both married and celibate – reconciled with their sexuality.'

His views are typical of many married convert Anglican clergymen who now serve as Catholic priests. Most are nervous as being presented as a kind of blueprint for the future of the Catholic priesthood. 'I have to recognize that there are things a celibate priest can do which I can't. I must not, for example, treat my wife and family as a sideshow, with my commitment as a priest something that squeeze them out. I do think, however, that the two roles are reconcilable.

'It depends on your theological basis – if you think that being connected with God means being unconnected with other human beings. This sets up a rivalry between love for God and love for human beings, and that is not what the gospel is about.'

Eastern Rite Catholic Churches

There are several Eastern Rite Catholic Churches, many based on the ancient patriarchates of Alexandria, Antioch, Constantinople and Jerusalem, which have remained in full communion with Rome. Together, they are believed to account for around 12 million Catholics worldwide. These Churches have their own liturgical traditions and, in most, priests can marry. The principal Eastern Rite Churches are:

▶ **The Armenian Catholic Church:** established in full communion with Rome by Pope Benedict XIV in 1742, a breakaway from the Armenian Apostolic (Orthodox) Church, which uses the Armenian Rite, with principal centres in Armenia, Lebanon, Syria, Poland and the United States.

▶ **The Chaldean Catholic Church:** also known as the Chaldean Church of Babylon, and linked with Rome since the fifteenth century, after a split in the Assyrian Church of the East, but in full communion only since 1830. With 600,000 members in Iraq, Iran and Australia, headed by the Patriarch of Babylon of the Chaldeans, who is also a cardinal.

▶ **The Coptic Catholic Church:** the result of a schism within the Coptic Orthodox Church, this 243,000-member Church is mainly based in Upper Egypt, uses the Alexandrian Rite and has been headed since 1895 by the Coptic Catholic Patriarch of Alexandria.

▶ **The Ethiopian Catholic Church:** developed out of a schism with the Ethiopian Orthodox Church, but distinct from Latin Rite Churches in the region because its Ethiopic Rite uses the ancient and otherwise little-used Semitic Ge'ez language. Fewer than 1 per cent of Ethiopians are members.

▶ **The Greek Catholic Church:** a group of closely related Churches spread throughout Eastern Europe and the Balkans, using the Byzantine Rite, which split from Orthodoxy from the seventeenth century onwards.

▶ **The Maronite Church:** founded by the fifth-century monk and mystic Saint Maron, who lived and died as a hermit on Mount Lebanon. This tradition within Catholicism numbers 3.5 million members worldwide, with 1.25 million forming a powerful Christian presence in Lebanon.

▶ **The Melkite Catholic Church:** another largely Lebanese Eastern Rite Church, linked with the other Greek Catholic Churches, using Arabic in the liturgy, with 1.3 million members.

▶ **The Syriac Catholic Church:** based in Syria, on the ancient patriarchate of Antioch, the result of a split in the Syriac Orthodox Church, but still using the same Antiochene rites.

▶ **The Syro-Malabar Catholic Church:** the largest of the Eastern Rite Churches, with 3.8 million adherents, tracing their roots back to Saint Thomas the Apostle who, legend has it, arrived in India in AD 52 and was martyred in AD 72.

▶ **The Syro-Malankara Catholic Church:** a breakaway group of around 500,000 members from the Syro-Malabar Catholic Church.

Priestly titles

Most Catholic priests are known simply as 'Father'. 'Reverend' tends to be an Anglican form of address, though Anglican priests who belong to the Anglo-Catholic tradition usually choose to be called Father.

Two other titles used by Catholic priests are 'Monsignor' and 'Canon'. 'Monsignor' dates back to the fourteenth century and can be used for any high-ranking clergyman – a cardinal, archbishop or bishop – as an alternative to other titles. When used of a priest, though, it denotes that he has been appointed by the Pope to one of three specific and honorary offices, by way of recognition for his ministry:

▶ Protonotary Apostolic (or honorary member of the Curia), which is restricted to priests over the age of 55 with more than 20 years since their ordination.

▶ Prelate of Honour (to the Pope), restricted to those over 45 with 15 years' service.

▶ Chaplain of Honour to the Pope, restricted to those over 35, with 10 years' service.

In April 2013 Pope Francis suspended the granting of the title of 'Monsignor' – except to members of the Holy See's diplomatic service – and in December of the same year announced that he would accept no further requests from bishops for appointments of monsignors apart from among the third category of Chaplains of Honour to the Pope. Even in this case, he said, any candidate would have to be over 65. His intention, it was said, was to abolish such honours as part of his drive against 'clerical careerism'.

The title of 'Canon' originally referred to priests who lived next to, or in the precinct of, a cathedral and who played a role in its administration. This remains one reason for having the title 'Canon' today, but there are also two other types among the Catholic priesthood – those who belong to religious orders of canons (rather than brothers) and those who have been given the honorary title of Canon by the diocesan bishop, in recognition of many years' service in a parish or elsewhere.

Key idea

If in doubt, address a priest as Father.

Religious life

'With his life and work, Saint Benedict exercised a fundamental influence on the development of European civilization and culture.'
Pope Benedict XVI, speaking in April 2008

Of the total number of Catholic priests in the world, it is estimated that some 65 per cent are 'diocesan' – that is, working with their local bishop as part of the diocesan team, having trained in the diocesan seminary – and 35 per cent belong to religious orders. They may well be doing exactly the same work as diocesan priests, but owe their first allegiance to their order.

Religious orders have been part of Catholicism since the Desert Fathers of the third century. Members live in communities, based on the model of Jesus and his Apostles. If the first centuries of the Church were dominated by the prospect and, often, the reality of martyrdom, then, once the Roman Empire accepted Christianity, some felt the need to find new and radical ways to answer Jesus' call in baptism to lead pure lives. They found it in monasticism.

Saint Antony (251–356) is regarded by Catholicism as the founder of monasticism. He gathered other like-minded individuals to join loose-knit communities of hermits in the Egyptian desert. They would spend their time in prayer, study and hard labour, focusing on Jesus' example when he spent 40 days and 40 nights in the desert and, like him, resisting the temptations put in their path by the Devil.

They attracted many admirers, among them Benedict of Nursia (480–547). He was so appalled by the excesses of life in Rome, where he had been sent to study, that he lived first as a hermit and then within a community of monks. Around 529 he established the monastery at Monte Cassino, 80 miles south of Rome, and drew up his Rule – or guide to monastic living – which has become the bedrock of Western monasticism in the Catholic Church.

1 The first degree of humility is obedience without delay. This is the virtue of those who hold nothing dearer to them than Christ; who, because of the holy service they have professed, and the fear of hell, and the glory of life everlasting, as soon as anything has been ordered by the Superior, receive it as a divine command and cannot suffer any delay in executing it.

2 Since the spirit of silence is so important, permission to speak should be rarely granted, even to perfect disciples, even though it be for good, holy, edifying conversation.

3 Let no one presume to give or receive anything without the Abbot's leave, or to have anything as his own since they are not permitted to have even their bodies or wills at their own disposal.

4 Then are they truly monastics when they live by the labour of their hands, as did our Fathers and the Apostles.

5 When we wish to suggest our wants to persons of high station, we do not presume to do so except with humility and reverence. How much the more, then, are complete humility and pure devotion necessary in supplicating the Lord who is God of the universe!

6 Let them sleep clothed and girded with belts and cords – but not with knives at their sides, lest they cut themselves in their sleep – and thus be always ready to rise without delay when the signal is given and hasten to be before one another at the word of God, yet with all gravity and decorum.

The religious charism

Not all members of religious orders are priests. Benedict wasn't, for example, and neither were those who, much later, joined the Congregation of Christian Brothers, founded in Ireland in the 1820s by Edmund Rice, and noted for their work in schools around the English-speaking world. But all members of religious orders do take vows of chastity, poverty and obedience, in imitation of Jesus. They live in a community, which is, in effect, their family.

All orders and congregations have what is known as a 'charism' – or unique aim – laid down by their founder. At the Second Vatican Council, they were told to return to those charisms, a process that saw many orders undergoing a major overhaul, changing their style of dress, their way of life and their work, for example, by withdrawing from running fee-paying schools or private hospitals in the developed world and focusing instead on the unanswered needs of the marginalized in their own societies, or in the developing world.

Most of the religious orders of the Catholic Church will have at their core one of the following traditions:

▶ **Augustinian** There are today five main branches of the Augustinian family, following variations on the Rule of Saint Augustine of Hippo. Distinguishing characteristics include an emphasis on truth and learning ('Nothing conquers except truth and the victory of truth is love,' Augustine wrote) and on music ('To sing once is to pray twice' is another maxim of Augustine's). Augustinians have been heavily involved in missionary work and include both mendicant – that is, rejecting property and living on charity – and lay branches. In the lay fraternities and societies (for women), individuals can live out the Augustinian rule as part of their daily secular lives.

▶ **Benedictine** Saint Benedict's Rule emphasizes peace, prayer, *lectio divina* (meditative reading) and work. It calls on monks to be part of 'a school for the Lord's service' and lays down key virtues of obedience to the abbot (or head of the community) and moderation. The various branches of the Benedictine family include both male and female groups, united under the Order of Saint Benedict, as well as independent orders following the Benedictine Rule, such as the Congregation of Cluny, the Cistercians and the Trappists. There are also Anglican and Orthodox Orders of Saint Benedict.

▶ **Dominican** Growing out of the Augustinian Rule, the Dominicans – or Order of Preachers, to give them their correct title – were founded in 1216 by Dominic de Guzman (1170–1221) in southern France. Dominic rejected the pomp and wealth of the papacy and insisted instead on 'zealous speaking', 'apostolic humility' and 'austerity'. The combination of the active life – preaching the gospel – and the contemplative – study and prayer – is at the heart of the Dominican tradition. From originally staffing the Inquisition, the Dominicans are among Catholicism's foremost intellectuals. They eschew the large monasteries of other orders and are mendicants, relying on charitable hand-outs to fund their work.

▶ **Carmelite** The tradition of the Carmelites holds that their origins lay in a community of hermits founded in the twelfth century on Mount Carmel in Israel by Saint Bertold (d.1195), a former Crusader. Their rule stresses the central role of prayer and includes great Marian devotion. Many Carmelite communities are enclosed – shut off from the world and dedicated to silence, contemplation and prayer (often for the world). There are also active branches. Saint Teresa of Ávila (1515–82) led a successful reform of the order in the sixteenth century, returning it to its original charism of poverty and rejection of worldly values and founding the Discalced Carmelites.

▶ **Franciscan** The Rule of Saint Francis of 1223 lies at the heart of the three modern branches of the Franciscan family. All follow the example of their founder, Saint Francis of Assisi (1181–1226), in embracing poverty so as to work with the most needy. Originally, Saint Francis set up his Order of Friars Minor to mitigate the sufferings of the urban poor, feeling that the older religious orders in their grand monasteries had abandoned them. The Franciscans were traditionally fierce defenders of the papacy and staffed the Inquisition.

▶ **Jesuit** The Jesuits are today the largest male religious order in Catholicism with (in 2007) 19,216 members. They were founded in Paris by Ignatius Loyola as the Company of Jesus in 1534, receiving papal approval as the Society of Jesus in 1540. Working in education, making converts and resisting the encroachments of Protestantism, the Jesuits had a quasi-military organization that earned them the title 'the foot soldiers of the Pope' in the Counter-Reformation years. They spread around the globe, being prominent in the missions. Their key text is Ignatius's *Spiritual Exercises*.

At different stages in Catholicism's history, religious orders have wielded great influence in the Church, but have also suffered periods of decline. There was, for example, a burst of growth in the mid-nineteenth century, with many orders founded to do apostolic work in schools, hospitals and the overseas missions. In just three years, between 1862 and 1865, Pope Pius IX approved the establishment of 74 new religious orders for women.

Since the Second Vatican Council, with many orders struggling to reconcile their founding charism with their historic role, there has been a general exodus from the religious orders, especially in the developed world. Research from Fordham University on the situation in the USA gives a snapshot of the issues faced. In 1965 there were, it reports, 3,559 Jesuit seminarians. By the year 2000 that figure had dropped to 389. In the Christian Brothers, the figures for the same period fall from 912 to just 7.

However, there has been a corresponding growth in the developing world. The religious orders see this as proof that their charisms still have great appeal for Catholics, though it is worth considering how far they are attracting recruits – as once they did in Europe – because they can offer young men and women who would otherwise go without an education the possibility of study in a secure and structured environment.

Dig deeper

Peter King, *Western Monasticism: A History* (Cistercian Press, 1999).

Douglas Letson and Michael Higgins, *The Jesuit Mystique* (Macmillan, 1995).

James Martin, *The Jesuit Guide to (Almost) Everything* (Harper, 2012).

Uta Ranke Heinemann, *Eunuchs for Heaven: The Catholic Church and Sexuality* (André Deutsch, 1990).

Julian Stead, *Saint Benedict: A Rule for Beginners* (New City Press, 2012).

Fact-check

1 Which political offices can today's priests hold?
   a Member of Parliament
   b Government minister
   c Cabinet minister
   d None

2 At what age do bishops have to tender their resignation?
   a 65
   b 70
   c 75
   d 80

3 What colour do bishops wear?
   a Purple
   b Scarlet
   c White
   d Orange

4 What is a coadjutor bishop?
   a An assistant bishop
   b The current bishop's eventual successor
   c The previous bishop
   d A retired bishop

5 For the first thousand years of Christianity what did a candidate for ordination to the priesthood have to demonstrate?
   a Virtue
   b Celibacy
   c Chastity
   d Virginity

6 Which of the following can a deacon *not* do?
   a Conduct baptisms
   b Consecrate the Eucharist
   c Conduct marriages
   d Conduct funerals

7 Where are vocations to the priesthood rising at the fastest rate?
   a Africa
   b Asia
   c The Americas
   d Europe

8 Where was Benedict's first monastery?
   a Florence
   b Assisi
   c Rome
   d Monte Cassino

9 In Benedict's Rule what is *lectio divina*?
   a A holy book
   b Essential reading
   c Divine prayers
   d Meditative reading

10 Who founded the Dominicans?
   a Dominic de Guzman
   b Ignatius Loyola
   c Francis of Assisi
   d Dominic Savio

Women in the Church

In this chapter you will learn:

▶ *about the role of nuns*
▶ *why women can't be priests*
▶ *of Catholicism's most celebrated nuns.*

The attitude of Catholicism to women is often debated, principally because, by continuing to reserve the ordained ministry to men, the Church goes against secular trends to treat men and women as equal. Changing attitudes on women priests in other Christian Churches have further concentrated attention on this issue. In 1994 the Church of England decided to permit the ordination of women, and in January 2015 appointed its first woman bishop. In 2006 the Episcopal (Anglican) Church in the United States elected as its leader Bishop Katharine Jefferts Schori, who was raised a Catholic.

One of the features of Catholicism, however, is its reluctance to follow what the rest of the world is doing or thinking, and so it has rebutted forcibly the argument that it should grant absolute equality for men and women before God. Yes, the Catholic Church has said, men and women are equal, but they are also different. This view has been put forward with great persistence by recent popes, most notably John Paul II who had a great devotion to Mary, the mother of Jesus, and who often held her up as the supreme role model for women.

Spotlight

Many Catholic feminists, in favour of women's ordination, respect the Virgin Mary's special position in Catholicism, even if they question attempts by the hierarchy to use Mary to argue that women should be content with a different role from men's. Mary's example is capable of many interpretations.

Women priests

The Catholic Church teaches that women cannot be ordained as priests. The most recent, and clearest, restatement of that teaching was 1994's Apostolic Letter *Ordinatio Sacerdotalis* ('On Ordination to the Priesthood'). It was released by John Paul II under his ordinary *magisterium* – or teaching authority – so he was not speaking *ex cathedra* (from the throne), using his extraordinary *magisterium*, and so the teaching cannot be considered infallible under the terms agreed by the cardinals in 1870. However, the Vatican was anxious at the time to stress that this was a final and definitive statement on the matter.

It moved to discourage wider discussion of the matter. So when, in 1994, a British nun, Sister Lavinia Byrne, published *Women at the Altar*, a book on the history of female ministry in the Church, touching on the archaeological evidence for women priests in the early Church, the Vatican insisted that official Church publishing houses withdraw the book. Byrne was later to leave her religious order.

Key idea

Catholicism teaches that women cannot be priests. Furthermore, it discourages discussion of the issue.

Evidence for women priests in the early Church

The evidence includes:

- ▶ inscriptions on mid-fifth-century tombstones in southern Italy and Calabria referring to *presbiteras* – or women priests

- ▶ a letter written by Pope Gelasius I (492–6) to Catholics in southern Italy recounting reports of 'women officiating at sacred altars and all matters reserved for the male sex'

- ▶ fifth-century mosaics in the ancient Roman basilica of St Praxedes, which stands on the site of one of the meeting places of the first Christians in the city, showing four women, one of whom is described as 'Theodora Episcopa' – 'Theodora, the woman bishop'

▶ in the Catacomb of St Priscilla in Rome, where first-century Christians hid from their Roman persecutors, an early third-century fresco showing seven figures, one if not all of them women, celebrating the Eucharist by re-enacting the Last Supper.

The official reaction to such archaeological and historical evidence is to point out that Pope Gelasius was, in his letter, clearly intent on outlawing women priests in southern Italy, that Theodora was the mother of Pope Paschal I (817–24) and therefore was being called a bishop as a mark of respect to him, and that – in the words of the Vatican Commission on Sacred Archaeology – the fresco in the catacombs may show women at the Eucharist, but that it is a man (albeit in a veil) who is actually breaking the bread.

Objections to women priests

Catholicism's objections to women priests are that:

▶ Jesus chose only men as his Apostles

▶ the priest represents Jesus, who was incarnated on earth as a man

▶ there is no tradition within the Church of women priests.

Some feminists have suggested that to this list might also be added that Catholicism regards women as second-class citizens, but Pope John Paul II was anxious to dispel any such impression. In his 1988 Apostolic Letter *Mulieris Dignitatem* ('On the Dignity of Women'), for example, he wrote: 'The Church gives thanks for each and every woman: for mothers, for sisters, for wives, for women consecrated to God in virginity.' He argued that women were the equal of men, but different from them. 'In the name of liberation from male domination, women must not appropriate to themselves male characteristics contrary to their own feminine originality. There is a well-founded fear that if they take this path they will... deform and lose what constitutes this essential richness.'

In his 1995 *Letter to Women*, he emphasized women's role as mothers, bringing 'God's own smile upon the newborn child, the one who guides your child's first steps, who helps it to grow, and who is the anchor as the child makes its way along the journey of life.' He also applauded women who have careers and bemoaned the fact that for so long women had been 'relegated to the margins of society and even reduced to servitude'.

And Pope Francis has made the promotion of women to senior roles in the Curia a priority of his papacy. He has been outspoken in praising the faith of women – and often comparing it favourably with that of men. In his general audience in April 2013 the Pope noted how, in the gospels, it is women who were the first witnesses of the Resurrection, adding that, 'The Apostles and disciples find it harder to believe in the Risen Christ, not the women, however!'

Those who argue in favour of women priests describe Jesus' decision to choose only male Apostles as dictated by the context of his times. Women were rarely seen in public roles in the society in which he lived. But in *Ordinatio Sacerdotalis* John Paul II rejected this proposition, pointing out that, had he wanted a female Apostle, Jesus could have included his mother.

Key idea

Catholicism holds up the Virgin Mary as its pre-eminent role model for women.

Repeatedly in their teachings, popes have used the Virgin Mary as a role model for women. While her virginity, even after giving birth, her freedom from the stain of original sin, and her assumption body and soul into heaven, may all set her apart from other women, Catholicism teaches that her example should guide and inspire her sex.

'The Church sees in Mary the highest expression of the "feminine genius" and she finds in her a source of constant inspiration. Mary called herself the "handmaid of the Lord". Through obedience to the word of God she accepted her lofty yet not easy vocation as wife and mother in the family of Nazareth. Putting herself at God's service, she also put herself at the

> *service of others: a service of love. Precisely through this service Mary was able to experience in her life a mysterious, but authentic reign. It is not by chance that she is invoked as "Queen of heaven and earth". The entire community of believers thus invokes her; many nations and peoples call upon her as their "Queen". For her, "to reign" is to serve! Her service is "to reign".'*
>
> Pope John Paul II In his 1995 *Letter to Women*

From 2004 onwards, a small group of American, German, Austrian and South African Catholic women who wanted to be priests started to challenge the authorities. They were first ordained as priests by bishops, some of whom were in good standing with the Vatican, but others who had fallen out with it. Then three of these women were consecrated bishops by other male bishops who have never been named (because, the women claim, they will be persecuted by the Vatican if they are). The new women bishops have subsequently ordained a number of other Catholic women as priests. On several occasions the ordinations have taken place on a riverboat, so as to avoid falling under the jurisdiction of the local Catholic bishop.

The women argue that their ordination is legitimate because it is linked back to male bishops who are in their turn linked back through the Church to Saint Peter himself. The Vatican, however, has rejected this, saying that the male bishops involved had no authority whatsoever to overturn the Pope's ruling, and by doing so risk excommunication.

Spotlight

In 2006 I interviewed one of the women priests for a British newspaper. Victoria Rue from California was in Britain to meet members of the pressure group Catholic Women's Ordination. In her ministry on a university campus in the States, she believed herself to be spearheading a historic change in Catholicism: 'The local bishop sent a letter to Catholics saying I was an invalid priest. That was wonderful publicity. A crowd turned up to see me. A lot of them have stayed on. Once they experience us, they know there is nothing to fear. Poll after poll of American Catholics shows that a majority wants women priests. The Vatican is refusing to listen right now but how much longer it can go on doing that, I don't know.'

Nuns

The term 'nun' is associated in popular Western culture principally with Catholicism, though there are also Anglican, Orthodox, Lutheran, Jain, Buddhist and Taoist nuns. In Catholicism, there is a distinction between a nun and a religious sister, although the terms are often used interchangeably, albeit sometimes inaccurately. In general, a nun has taken solemn vows and is usually a member of an order and often lives in an enclosed community. A religious sister, by contrast, is a member of an Institute or Congregation of sisters, has taken simple vows, and usually is involved in practical work in the community. Benedictine nuns are traditionally known as Dames – the female equivalent of Dom, used for Benedictine monks – but this practice is now dying out.

In the decades since the Second Vatican Council, the number of nuns has dropped sharply throughout the Western world. According to a study by Fordham University, there has been a decline in the USA from a peak of 180,000 in 1965 to just 75,000 in 2002 and a projected 40,000 in 2020. Many of the smaller orders – particularly those founded to work in schools or hospitals in the eighteenth and nineteenth centuries – have now gone many years in developed countries without attracting any new vocations. Most, however, have also seen growth in numbers in the developing world and have progressively moved their centres of operations there.

Spotlight

There is sadness for members of many smaller religious orders in the West who find themselves managing decline and eventual closure. They joined as one of many, part of a chain that they believed would stretch forwards as well as backwards. Now many must come to terms with being the last of the line, in their country.

Even the contemplative orders such as the Carmelites and Benedictines – traditionally more successful in attracting vocations in recent times – have seen numbers dwindle in the West. Only the Missionaries of Charity, established in 1950 by the late Mother Teresa of Calcutta, with their distinctive blue-and-white habits, have seen a growth in vocations all around the globe.

To the vows of chastity, poverty and obedience, the Missionaries of Charity add a fourth – 'wholehearted and free service to the poorest of the poor'. With a rigid structure, and a great emphasis on prayer and active work, the order has little time for study or self.

The appeal of the Missionaries of Charity is much discussed, partly in the hope that other orders can learn from it. One factor seems to be the challenge of the demands it makes on those who join. They must give up all worldly comforts and live the simplest life in material terms. The order is determinedly practical and anti-intellectual. If members are busy doing, they have less opportunity to dwell on doubts and debates over doctrine.

Key idea

In April 2015 the English and Welsh Church announced that the number of women entering religious life had risen to 45, a 25-year high. The figure, though, is still tiny compared to numbers 50 years ago.

A history of service

Women dedicating their lives to prayer and service have been part of Christianity from the earliest of days. Saint Paul, in the First Letter of to the Corinthians (7:34–5). urged unmarried women to devote themselves 'to the Lord's affairs; all [they] need worry about is being holy in body and spirit'.

By the third century there is evidence of communities of women turning their backs on sexual relations and dedicating themselves to God. In the fourth century the wealthy widow Saint Paula (347–404) established a communal house for women in

Bethlehem, where they would offer a welcome to pilgrims to the city and cared for Saint Jerome who had settled nearby.

With the growth of monasticism in the West under Benedict and his followers, female monasteries were established where women would take vows of chastity, poverty and obedience and wear long, simple garments that covered the body, and a headdress or wimple that left only the face visible. Often, male and female houses would exist side by side but separate, sometimes presided over by female abbesses such as the renowned Hilda of Whitby (614–80).

Hilda was the great niece of a king. Other abbesses who enjoyed similar authority over men were often high born, but the Church distrusted their independence. By the twelfth century, when Saints Francis and Dominic were establishing orders of travelling friars and preachers, efforts to set up the female equivalent, for instance by Saint Clare in 1215, were restricted by the demand from the papacy that the women should live under enclosure – within a convent – for their own safety. They were allowed to travel outside the walls, but this freedom was strictly curtailed in the centuries ahead.

It was not until the seventeenth century, in 1633, when the Sisters of Charity were established in France, that religious sisters were permitted to serve the community by living without enclosure. Another pioneer in this area was Mary Ward, who founded the Institute of the Blessed Virgin Mary, a teaching order with a Jesuit style of spirituality. One of the few activities that could be carried out within the rules of enclosure had been teaching, and this was now able to spread outward throughout Catholicism. The tradition of nun teachers providing education to girls who would otherwise have no access to it goes back many centuries.

The enclosure did, however, have great appeal as a place of safety where women were permitted both to govern themselves and to study, something often denied them elsewhere. The experiment of Beguinage in the Low Countries in the thirteenth century, with houses of learning for religious women that were not enclosed, had struggled in the face of male hostility.

Spotlight

A community of Beguines flourished in the Singel district of Amsterdam from the fourteenth century onwards. The tradition endured through many periods of change and upheaval. The last Beguine to live there, Sister Antonia, died in 1971 at the age of 84, and the enclosed courtyard, called the Begijnhof, can still be visited.

In the eighteenth and nineteenth centuries, there was rapid growth in the number of active female orders. Their decline in the twentieth century, however, was just as rapid. In the clerical/lay divide of Catholicism before the Second Vatican Council, nuns were classified as laity and were often expected to perform secondary, assistant roles to priests. Since the Council, however, they have been encouraged to modernize their dress and return to their founding charisms so as to reassess where they should be concentrating their work. Nonetheless, worldwide, according to official statistics, the number of nuns continues to fall. In 2012 there were 710,000 compared to 970,000 in 1975.

Case study: The LCWR

In 2008 Pope Benedict ordered an 'apostolic visitation' – or Vatican inspection – of the 400 or so congregations of nuns in the United States to look into claims that they had become too radical in their outlook and were not faithfully following Church teaching. It was a controversial move, with some of the 50,000 nuns in America objecting that it had been issued in patriarchal tones. Some refused to complete questionnaires sent to them by Rome and others even refused to meet the inspectors.

Tensions rose further in 2012 when the Vatican issued a reprimand to the Leadership Conference of Women Religious (LCWR), a high-profile group of the senior figures in female orders and congregations in the States. It accused the LCWR of spending too much time helping the poor, and not enough on promoting Church teaching on marriage and sexuality. It also described the LCWR as being 'silent on the right to life' because it had not taken a more outspoken stance on the long-running campaign in the United States to ban abortion.

However, the election of Pope Francis in 2013 changed the whole tone of the debate between the women religious and the Vatican. He made combatting poverty his priority, and so in December 2014 the inspection process was ended with the publication of a Vatican report that contained only the mildest criticisms. It called on American nuns to 'carefully review their spiritual practices and ministry to assure that these are in harmony with Catholic teaching about God, creation, the incarnation and the redemption'.

Ten significant nuns

BLESSED TERESA (1910–97)

Known in her lifetime as Mother Teresa of Calcutta, this Albanian-born nun, trained in Ireland, was based in India from 1929, initially as a teacher with the Institute of the Blessed Virgin Mary. In 1946 she experienced 'a call within a call' to serve the poorest of the poor, those she identified as 'the hungry, the naked, the homeless, the crippled, the blind, the lepers, all those people who feel unwanted, unloved, uncared for throughout society, people that have become a burden to the society and are shunned by everyone'. In 1950 the Missionaries of Charity were given official approval and later a male branch was established. In 1979 Mother Teresa received the Nobel Peace Prize for her work, and by the time of her death there were 4,000 sisters working in 123 countries. Pope John Paul II beatified her in 2002.

SAINT THÉRÈSE OF LISIEUX (1873–97)

Known as 'the Little Flower', this French Carmelite is associated with the 'Little Way' approach to living out faith and spirituality, which focuses on the importance of small deeds. 'Great deeds are forbidden me,' she wrote. 'The only way I can prove my love is by scattering flowers, and these flowers are every little sacrifice, every glance and word, and the doing of the least actions for love.' She suffered ill health throughout her life, which she bore gladly, dying at the age of 24. After her death, her spiritual journal, *The Story of a Soul*, became a bestseller.

Spotlight

Relics of Thérèse – portions of her bones, contained in an elaborate casket or reliquary – have been touring France since 1947 and the world since 1997. They always draw large crowds. It is estimated that, in Ireland in 2002, 70 per cent of the population went to pray in front of the reliquary.

MARY WARD (1585–1645)

The English founder of the Institute of the Blessed Virgin Mary, also known as the Loreto Sisters and today as the Congregation of Jesus, was regarded as too radical in her day. She tried contemplative life but preferred running a school for rich and poor girls in St-Omer in France. Her efforts to set up an Institute without enclosure, obligation to attend choir, a habit or control by the local bishop, were controversial. Though her communities spread, they were suppressed by the papacy in 1630, only reviving 73 years later and growing into a force in the education of young women worldwide.

SAINT TERESA OF ÁVILA (1515–82)

A high-born Spaniard, she entered the Carmelites as a teenager, in the face of family opposition, but experienced long periods of ill health. She was also a mystic who saw visions – spiritual ecstasies – which led some to suspect she was possessed. With John of the Cross, she led a radical reform movement within the Carmelites, believing the order to have become too lax. Her work culminated in the establishment of the Discalced Carmelites – so called because they abandoned leather or wooden sandals and went barefoot.

SAINT CATHERINE OF SIENA (1347–80)

This Italian theologian and mystic rejected life in an enclosed convent to become a lay member of the Dominicans and to live, alone, as an anchoress in the world, dedicating herself to prayer, fasting and mortification of her flesh. In 1366 she had a vision which she described as a 'mystical marriage' with Jesus and thereafter dedicated herself to the service of the poorest. She had many subsequent visions and died, like Jesus, at the age of 33.

MOTHER JULIAN (1342–1416)

This medieval mystic and spiritual writer from Norwich, England, was a Benedictine nun who lived out her life as an anchoress, walled into a cell in the city church of St Julian from which she took her name. Her *Revelation of Divine Love* is believed to be the first book written in English by a woman and contains the phrase that sums up her spiritual insight: 'All shall be well, and all shall be well, and all manner of things shall be well.'

SAINT ELIZABETH OF HUNGARY (1207–31)

One of the few female saints in Catholicism to have been married and to have had children, Elizabeth was a king's daughter who was betrothed at the age of four to Louis IV of Thuringia. Inspired by Francis of Assisi, she began doing charitable works, freed to act by her royal status. On the death of her husband when she was 20, she resisted attempts to force her to remarry and became a lay Franciscan, founding a hospital for the poor and sick.

SAINT CLARE OF ASSISI (1194–1253)

Clare was one of the first followers of Francis of Assisi and, like him, embraced radical poverty as part of her commitment to the poor. She escaped from her family's demand that she should marry and founded a convent at San Damiano, following a Franciscan rule. Her sisters cut their hair short and wore rough tunics, but were unable to follow their male counterparts in travelling to tend the poor and sick, having, as women, to stay in the enclosure.

SAINT HILDEGARD OF BINGEN (1098–1179)

This remarkable German polymath gave her life to the Church from the age of eight, going on to found a monastery for women at Bingen on the Rhine. She composed music and wrote poems, theological, medical and botanical tracts.

SAINT HILDA OF WHITBY (614–80)

This royal-born abbess was part of the tradition of Celtic monasticism which spread from Ireland, via Iona in Scotland, to the 'new' Christian lands of England. In 657 she founded a double monastery on the banks of the river Wear, with separate houses for men and women living out their beliefs in peace, charity and biblical study. Her reputation as a teacher led to the holding of the first synod of the English Church, at Whitby in 664.

Consecrated virgins

> 'Similar to these forms of consecrated life is the order of virgins, who, committed to the holy plan of following Christ more closely, are consecrated to God by the diocesan bishop according to the approved liturgical rite, are betrothed mystically to Christ, the Son of God, and are dedicated to the service of the Church.'
>
> Canon 604 in the Catholic Church's *Code of Canon Law*

From the earliest times of Christianity, according to Saint Paul, there were unmarried women and widows who consecrated their lives to God and to the service of others. In his First Letter to Timothy (5:9) Paul suggests that the widow 'can give herself up to God and consecrate all her days and nights to petitions and prayer. The one who thinks only of pleasure is already dead while she is still alive.'

However, this ancient practice fell into disuse with the rise of women's religious orders. The Second Vatican Council restored it. Since 1970 Catholicism has laid down once again a solemn rite in which women can pledge their perpetual virginity as 'a transcendent sign of the Church's love for Christ'.

Some consecrated virgins form themselves into associations. Others use the freedom their choice has given them to live as hermits or solitaries. Some – like the art critic and popular religious broadcaster Sister Wendy Beckett – are also nuns, but live separately from the orders they originally joined.

Key idea

The Catholic Church continues to place a high value on those women as well as men who choose to abstain from sexual relationships.

Conclusion

Though the Second Vatican Council sought to abandon the distinction between clergy and laity, it remains one of the features of contemporary Catholicism. However, old barriers have gone and, with the decline in vocations, there is much more co-operation, even at the highest levels of the Catholic Church, than ever there was. Those who suggest permitting the ordination of married men and women to the priesthood are, their critics say, missing the point. Not only would it go against the tradition of the Church, it would not reverse the fall in vocations. However, a contrary argument would question whether, when individuals – be they celibate women or married males and females – genuinely feel themselves called by God to a life of priestly service, that calling can be ruled unacceptable by the Catholic Church.

Dig deeper

Lavinia Byrne, *Woman at the Altar* (Mowbray, 1994).

Shirley du Boulay, *Teresa of Ávila* (Hodder, 1991).

Jo Ann Kay McNamara, *Sisters in Arms: Catholic Nuns through Two Millennia* (Harvard, 1996).

Anne Sebba, *Mother Teresa: Beyond the Image* (Weidenfeld & Nicolson, 1997).

Karen Jo Torjesen, *When Women Were Priests* (Harper, 1997).

Fact-check

1 Who does Catholicism hold up as the highest exponent of 'feminine genius'?
- **a** Mother Teresa of Calcutta
- **b** Mary Magdalen
- **c** The Virgin Mary
- **d** Eve

2 How were Benedictine nuns traditionally known?
- **a** Dame
- **b** Lady
- **c** Sister
- **d** Mother

3 Who founded the Missionaries of Charity?
- **a** Saint Clare of Assisi
- **b** Saint Elizabeth of Hungary
- **c** Mother Teresa of Calcutta
- **d** Pope Francis

4 Which of the following presided over a 'double' monastery of men and women religious?
- **a** Saint Paul
- **b** Hilda of Whitby
- **c** Julian of Norwich
- **d** Sister Wendy Beckett

5 What was unusual about the Sisters of Charity when they were founded in 1633?
- **a** All members were women
- **b** They lived in the desert
- **c** They were not enclosed
- **d** They went as missionaries to Africa

6 Mary Ward's Institute of the Blessed Virgin Mary was a ground-breaking organization in what field?
- **a** Female education
- **b** Music
- **c** Nursing
- **d** Silent prayer

7 Members of all-female religious communities in the Low Countries in the thirteenth century were known as what?

   a Nuns

   b Religious sisters

   c Dames

   d Beguines

8 In 2008 the Vatican ordered an inspection of the work of nuns in which country?

   a Italy

   b The Philippines

   c The United States

   d Germany

9 Who is best known as the 'Little Flower'?

   a Teresa of Ávila

   b Thérèse of Lisieux

   c Mother Teresa

   d Teresa of Portugal

10 Which of the following nuns was a medical pioneer in the twelfth century?

   a Catherine of Siena

   b Saint Paula

   c Elizabeth of Hungary

   d Hildegard of Bingen

Part Four

Teachings and traditions

The sacramental and devotional life of Catholics

In this chapter you will learn:

▶ *about distinctive Catholic liturgical traditions*

▶ *about transubstantiation*

▶ *about fish on Fridays.*

All faiths have their rites, rituals and distinctive, sometimes eye-catching, devotions. Catholicism is no exception. At its heart is the Mass and the Eucharist – for Catholics literally the bread of life. The other sacraments play an important part, though some more than others. And then there are devotions, some of long standing, rooted in the scriptures and the tradition of the Church. Not all have endured, and some have suffered a decline in popularity but are still associated in the public mind with Catholicism. Others have roots elsewhere but have become part of the fabric of Catholic life.

The Mass

The Catholic Church, instructs the *Catechism*, 'obliges the faithful to take part in the Divine Liturgy on Sundays'. This obligation can also be discharged by attending Mass on the evening of the previous day – that is, the Saturday. Exceptions are made in cases of serious illness or of heavy child-care responsibilities, particularly of infants, but absence otherwise is regarded as a grave sin. Despite this, Mass-going statistics for many hitherto staunchly Catholic countries in the developed world (for example, Ireland) have shown a fall in recent years in the numbers attending every Sunday without fail. The growing tendency to interpret what had once been seen as hard-and-fast rules, highlighted earlier in the wake of the publication of *Humanae Vitae*, seems to be having an effect in this area too.

Though the term 'Mass' to denote a standardized liturgy is believed to date back to the fifth century, there were Eucharistic celebrations recorded as early as the second century.

What the saint is describing will be familiar to all Catholics as the structure of the modern Mass. It consists of readings from the Old and New Testaments, and then from the gospels, a homily by the priest and intercessions – together known as the Liturgy of the Word – followed by the offering of gifts, the consecration of the bread and wine, the kiss of peace, and communion (the Liturgy of the Eucharist).

Spotlight

It is precisely the close connection between the modern Mass and those celebrated in the early years of the Church, and described by Justin Martyr, that draws Catholics to liturgy. It links them with a continuous thread of worship through two millennia.

As a whole, the form of the Mass imitates Jesus at the Last Supper, walking around the table (the altar in the Mass), explaining the scriptures to his Apostles, then breaking bread with them. The priest stands in the place of Christ.

Greater participation by the laity (the congregation) has been encouraged in recent years – as readers, in the presentation of the offerings at the Offertory, and as ministers of the Eucharist, assisting the priest in the distribution of the bread and wine, the body and blood of Christ. There have also been limits maintained on such participation. Only the priest, for instance, can read the gospel and, while lay members of the congregation can speak from the pulpit after the communion, the homily is usually reserved for priests.

Spotlight

Liturgical arrangements are one of the most contentious areas in Catholicism. Some Catholics complain that their faith needs to be lived out in the world, rather than 'performed' in a church, but the fact that debates on liturgy are so heated reveals how close it is to most Catholics' hearts.

The Eucharist

Catholics are obliged to receive the Eucharist at least once a year, if possible during the Easter season. Attendance at first the sacrament of reconciliation and then at the Eucharist is traditionally referred to as 'Easter duties'. The Catholic Church does not allow members of other faiths to receive communion at its Eucharistic celebrations (and discourages Catholics from doing so at those of other Christian denominations) because it holds that their understanding of Christ's real presence in the bread and wine is different from that in Catholicism.

Key idea

Catholics are required to receive the Eucharist at least once a year. Non-Catholics cannot receive Holy Communion at a Catholic service.

'The mode of Christ's presence under the Eucharistic species is unique,' the *Catechism* instructs. 'It raises the Eucharist above all the sacraments as the perfection of the spiritual life and the end to which all the sacraments tend.' Catholics believe that contained in the consecrated bread and wine are the body and blood of Christ, as well as his soul and divinity, 'truly, really and substantially'.

This belief is called transubstantiation and was an issue in the Reformation debates, and remained a key point of divergence in the talks that went on under the auspices of ARCIC – the Anglican Roman Catholic International Commission. Other Christian faiths tend to emphasize the symbolic nature of the bread and wine in the Eucharist. Catholicism goes considerably further. 'It is', the *Catechism* points out, 'presence in the fullest sense: that is to say, it is a substantial presence by which Christ, God and man, makes himself wholly and entirely present.'

Key idea

Catholicism believes that Jesus is present 'in the fullest sense' in the bread and wine offered in the Eucharist. This belief is called transubstantiation.

In the Eucharist, Catholicism believes, Christ is wholly and entirely present among the faithful. By receiving the unleavened bread or host, the bond with Jesus is strengthened. In John's gospel (6:55–7), Jesus tells those who doubt him: '...anyone who does eat my flesh and drink my blood has eternal life, and I shall raise him up on the last day. For my flesh is real food, and my blood is real drink. He who eats my flesh and drinks my blood lives in me and I live in him.'

Baptism

Catholics are encouraged to have their children baptised as soon as possible after birth. In the past this would have meant within a few days, but now it can be months. The Church used to teach that unbaptised children who died in infancy would spend eternal life in Limbo, a place of 'natural happiness' but away from the presence of God. The Vatican formally abandoned this concept in 2005.

> *'Limbo was never a defined truth of faith... I would abandon it, since it was only a theological hypothesis... It formed part of a secondary thesis in support of a truth which is absolutely of first significance for faith, namely, the importance of baptism.'*
>
> Benedict XVI, writing in 1985 when still Cardinal Joseph Ratzinger

In baptism, Catholics are cleansed by water of the stain of original sin – the legacy to humanity of Adam and Eve's disobedience in the Garden of Eden – and become members of the Church. Baptism, from the Greek word meaning to plunge or immerse, has been part of the Church from its earliest days. Jesus was baptized by his cousin, John the Baptist, and Saint Peter, in the Acts of the Apostles (2:38), made his first conversions, following Jesus' death, resurrection and ascension into heaven, with the words 'every one of you must be baptised in the name of Jesus Christ for the forgiveness of all your sins and you will receive the gift of the Holy Spirit.'

These words remain at the core of Catholicism's understanding of baptism. Part of the celebration of the sacrament is a form of exorcism. Either the adult to be baptised or the parents and godparents on behalf of an infant will formally reject Satan and all his ways. There will also be an anointing with chrism, or sacred oil, consecrated by a bishop, signifying the gift of the Holy Spirit. Infants will be wrapped in a white garment, symbolizing that they have 'put on Christ', as Saint Paul describes it in his Letter to the Galatians (3:27), and a candle, lit from the Easter candle, signifies that Christ, the light of the world, has entered the newly baptised.

Key idea

The baptism ceremony is one of the few occasions where reference is made to Satan in Catholic rites.

Adults who wish to be baptised as Catholics have first to undertake the distinct steps set out in the Rite of Christian Initiation of Adults. These preparations can take up to 12 months. Those who have already been baptised as Anglicans are not required to undergo a second baptism. After a period of instruction, they are received into the Catholic Church.

Reconciliation

Also known as penance or confession or the sacrament of conversion, reconciliation allows Catholics to confess their sins to a priest and receive absolution. Sins can be either 'mortal' – the more serious – or 'venial' – the everyday. Confession of venial sins is recommended but not obligatory. Confession of mortal sins is required of Catholics in order to prepare them to receive the Eucharist.

Catholicism teaches that only God has the power to forgive sins, but the priest acts in his place. Penitents may be asked to say a penance – usually made up of several prayers – and/or occasionally to undertake works for the poor and needy. They also have to promise to do their best to avoid sinning again.

There are different permitted formats for the sacrament. Traditionally it has taken place in a confessional box, with the priest and penitent separated by a grille and curtain, going through a set series of prayers and responses. In more recent times, there has been a move to more informal face-to-face conversations.

The Catholic Church regards anything said during the sacrament of reconciliation as private. The phrase 'the seal of the confessional' expresses the belief that what is said during the sacrament cannot be repeated elsewhere.

'Let the priest absolutely beware that he does not by word or sign or by any manner whatever in any way betray the sinner: but if he should happen to need wiser counsel let him cautiously seek the same without any mention of person. For whoever shall dare to reveal a sin disclosed to him in the tribunal of penance we decree that he shall be not only deposed from the priestly office but that he shall also be sent into the confinement of a monastery to do perpetual penance.'
Fourth Lateran Council (1215)

Even if a murderer has confessed, the priest cannot reveal his identity to the authorities. The priest can refuse absolution and is required to if he does not believe that there exists true contrition – described by the Church as being in mind and heart, and accompanied by sorrow for the deed or sin itself.

A priest may also, before granting absolution, require some other form of reparation other than the saying of prayers. In rare cases this may include contacting the relevant civil authorities if, for instance, a murderer is confessing.

Many dioceses have what are described as 'reserved sins' where a priest needs special permission from his bishop to grant absolution. These vary but can include abortion, murder or child abuse. If the priest does not have permission, the penitent must be referred to the local bishop.

Catholicism also allows for penance to take place within communal celebrations – with participants preparing themselves together and then giving thanks for the forgiveness they receive. The personal confession of sins and individual absolution are included within a liturgy of readings, an examination of conscience, and a communal request for forgiveness. Though such rites of general absolution were introduced into Catholicism in 1975, the Vatican has stressed repeatedly that they should only be used sparingly or in exceptional circumstances.

Spotlight

Though dramatists, screenwriters and novelists remain fond of the old-fashioned confessional box, with Catholics baring their soul to their priests through a thick purple curtain, in the real world this traditional form of the sacrament of reconciliation has been going out of fashion since my childhood.

First Holy Communion

First Holy Communion is one of the landmarks of any Catholic's life. Traditionally, girls will wear a white dress (to symbolize purity) for their first reception of the sacrament of Eucharist, though this has been discouraged in more recent times, with the Church anxious to concentrate candidates' minds on what is happening rather than how they are dressed.

In the earliest times of the Church, it was common for very small children to participate in the Eucharist from the time of their baptism. This is still the practice in some of the Eastern Rite Churches in communion with Rome. However, for most Catholics, since the Council of Tours in 813, First Holy Communion comes at around the age of seven or eight. This is when the child is judged capable of fuller participation in the sacramental life of the Church.

Preparation, by lay catechists (or teachers), is usually done in conjunction with that for first reconciliation. There has been some dispute over the centuries over this close connection between the two sacraments, with a body of opinion holding that, while it is possible for a child of eight to be sufficiently mature to receive the sacrament of penance, Eucharist should be delayed until the early teens because of its central importance in Catholic life. The Vatican has repeatedly rejected this argument.

Spotlight

British director Ken Loach's 1993 film *Raining Stones* won the Jury Prize at the Cannes Film Festival. It tells of how a proud but poor working-class Catholic father struggles to afford a traditional white First Holy Communion dress for his daughter, and how he becomes involved in criminal activities to pay for it.

Confirmation

Confirmation is regarded in Catholicism as an opportunity to mark an increase and deepening of God's grace, originally bestowed by baptism. It is an occasion when the presence in each individual of the Holy Spirit, first marked at baptism, is confirmed and the seven gifts of the spirit are bestowed to guide individuals through their adult lives.

The seven gifts of the Holy Spirit are based on an Old Testament passage (Isaiah 11:2–3) and have been defined by, among others, Saint Thomas Aquinas in his *Summa Theologica*. They are:

▶ wisdom

▶ knowledge

▶ counsel (also known as right judgement)

▶ fortitude (courage)

▶ understanding (common sense)

▶ piety

▶ fear of the Lord (wonder and awe in God).

Aquinas wrote that the first four concern the intellect and the remaining three the will towards God.

Confirmation is sometimes known as 'the sacrament of Christian maturity' and usually takes place when a young Catholic has reached the age of discretion in their early teens – though some Catholic dioceses have pioneered programmes where confirmation follows hard on the heels of First Holy Communion.

Confirmation is usually administered by the local bishop. Candidates, having completed a lengthy preparation, will each have a sponsor. The bishop will anoint the candidate's forehead with sacred chrism and say the words, 'Be sealed with the gift of the Holy Spirit.' Traditionally, candidates also choose a saint as their patron.

Key idea

Once confirmed, a Catholic is regarded as having made a mature commitment to the Church.

Marriage

'a free and mutual giving of self, experienced in tenderness...
a far cry from mere erotic attraction, which is pursued in
selfishness and soon fades away into wretchedness'
Marriage, as described in the Second Vatican Council document
Gaudium et Spes

The Catholic Church teaches that God instituted marriage. He created Adam and Eve, a man and a woman, out of love and called them to love each other. Marriage was the expression given to that love and God was part of the partnership.

The symbolism of marriage pervades Catholicism. The covenant between God and the people of Israel in the Old Testament is presented, for example, as a nuptial bond. Jesus performs his first miracle at a wedding feast in Cana, and nuns are often described as 'brides of Christ'.

Jesus mentions marriage explicitly in the gospels and his injunction against divorce is clear and remains strong in Catholic teaching. Catholicism does not, as a rule, permit second marriages, unless either one original spouse has died or the first marriage has been subjected to the annulment procedure (which is discussed in Chapter 11). Catholicism does not recognize divorce and those who do divorce, in the civil courts, and then remarry are, as a rule, unable to receive the Eucharist. In very rare circumstances, priests may agree to bless second marriages and waive the bar on going to communion.

The *Catechism* makes it plain that marriage is to be preferred to remaining single. Marriage, it states, is the antidote to 'self-absorption, egoism, pursuit of one's own pleasure, and [an opportunity] to open oneself to the other, to mutual aid and to self-giving'. Catholicism also teaches that marriage is the proper context for sex and for the bringing up of children.

When two Catholics marry, it is usual for the sacrament to be bestowed within a Nuptial Mass. The Church requires that they give their free consent. Traditionally, it has frowned on mixed marriages, requiring Catholics who marry non-Catholics to marry quietly and without great ceremony. This, however, is rarely the case today.

The current *Catechism* restricts itself to pointing out the potential pitfalls of 'disunity' in the marital home. It does, however, reiterate the practice of requiring the Catholic partner to a marriage to pledge to have any children of that marriage baptized and educated as Catholics. This is now more often expressed as a hope than as a demand.

> **Key idea**
>
> Catholicism sees marriage as a vital, God-given institution, and a commitment that is made for life. It frowns on divorce and second marriages.

Holy orders

The sacrament of holy orders is the means by which Catholicism passes on to a new generation the original mission entrusted by Jesus to his Apostles. The word 'orders' comes from the Roman term for a governing body. Hence ordination is the ceremony by which you join the governing body.

There are three degrees of the sacrament – the episcopate, the presbyterate and the diaconate (or bishops, priests and deacons). Bishops, the Church teaches, enjoy the fullest expression of the sacrament. Priests are their co-workers, but deacons exist to serve and assist. They are ministers but not priests. Often candidates for the priesthood will first be ordained as deacons, but since the Second Vatican Council the Catholic Church has brought back the permanent diaconate, opening it to married men, to create a group who can assist the priesthood with the distribution of Holy Communion, preaching, and presiding at funerals. There is a growing demand among those who support women's ordination for the permanent diaconate to be opened to women, as a first step in answering the vocation that many women feel they have.

Only bishops, as the successors of the Apostles, can confer the sacrament of holy orders. Since the Second Vatican Council, those who have received it are referred to as the ministerial priesthood, to be distinguished from the common priesthood of the faithful.

The sacrament of the anointing of the sick

Once popularly known as Extreme Unction, this sacrament was usually associated with anointing the dying, but today it aims to bring comfort and healing to anyone who is sick. It was recommended to all the faithful and was instituted, Catholicism teaches, by James, the Apostle and brother of Jesus. It follows time-honoured rituals in older faiths of the anointing of the sick with oils.

Today's sacrament, as set out by the Vatican in the Apostolic Constitution, *Sacram Unctionem Infirmorum*, issued by Pope Paul VI in 1972, consists of the anointing of seriously ill people on the forehead and hands with blessed oil made from olives and other plants. 'Through this holy anointing,' the priest or bishop says, 'may the Lord in his love and mercy help you with the grace of the Holy Spirit. May the Lord who frees you from sin save you and raise you up.' If the person recovers and then falls ill again at a later point, he or she can receive the sacrament more than once.

Other devotions

Outside of the sacraments, there is a variety of other devotions which have long been a part of Catholic life. Some are seen both inside and outside the Mass – for instance, making the sign of the cross as you enter a Catholic Church, with holy water from a stoup near the entrance. This is a form of cleansing and reminds Catholics of the baptismal vows. It is usual to genuflect – go down on one knee and make the sign of the cross – before the main altar of the church and the tabernacle, which contains the Blessed Sacrament. Most Catholic churches house a place where visitors can light candles as part of seeking God's help for themselves or others who are sick or who have died. These banks of candles are usually found in front of a statue of the Virgin Mary, who intercedes with God on behalf of humanity.

As well as these devotions, there are several that take the form of rituals outside the Mass.

The Rosary

> '...among the finest and most praiseworthy traditions of Christian contemplation'
> Pope John Paul II on the Rosary in October 2002

The word 'rosary' refers both to a set of devotional prayers and to the beads that are traditionally used while reciting those prayers. Rosary beads, as they are often called, have been in existence since at least the twelfth century. In 1166 Saint Rosalia, a descendant of Charlemagne who lived a hermit's life of prayer and fasting, was buried with a rosary in her hands. Modern sets of rosary beads consist of a string of 50 beads, gathered in groups of ten (decades). The beads are used to count off the prayers as a Catholic says the Rosary.

Each decade of the Rosary consists of one 'Our Father', ten 'Hail Mary's' and one 'Glory Be to the Father'. While reciting these prayers, either out loud or, more unusually, silently, Catholics are directed to meditate and reflect on three sets of mysteries – the Joyful, the Sorrowful and the Glorious. To these three, in 2002, Pope John Paul added an optional fourth – the Luminous. Each of the sets of mysteries consists of five themes, one for each decade as you go around the rosary beads.

THE JOYFUL MYSTERIES

1 **The Annunciation** – when the Angel Gabriel comes down to earth to tell Mary that she is to give birth to God's son.

2 **The Visitation** – when Mary's elderly, childless cousin Elizabeth visits her and shares Mary's news, as well as announcing her own miraculous pregnancy with the child who is to become John the Baptist.

3   The Nativity – the story of Jesus' birth in a stable.

4   **The Presentation of Jesus at the Temple** – when Jesus, still a small child, is taken by his parents, as required by Jewish law, to be presented at the Temple in Jerusalem and is greeted, according to Luke's gospel (2:22–40) by Simeon, who hails him as the Messiah in a prayer known today in Catholicism as the *Nunc Dimittis*.

5   **The Finding of Jesus in the Temple** – another episode recounted only by Luke (2:41–50) when the 12-year-old Jesus accompanies his mother and father to the Temple, falls into conversation with the elders, and is believed lost by his distraught parents.

THE SORROWFUL MYSTERIES

1   **The Agony in the Garden** – Jesus' torment in the Garden of Gethsemane before he is betrayed by Judas and arrested.

2   **The Scourging at the Pillar** – when Jesus is whipped on the orders of Pontius Pilate, the Roman governor.

3   **The Crowning with Thorns** – when his captors torment Jesus on account of his claim to kingship and place a crown of thorns on his head.

4   **The Carrying of the Cross** – the *via dolorosa*, or way of sorrow – Jesus' climb to the hill of Calvary.

5   The Crucifixion.

THE GLORIOUS MYSTERIES

1   The Resurrection.

2   **The Ascension** – of Jesus into heaven.

3   **The Descent of the Holy Spirit** – giving the Apostles courage after their leader finally left them.

4   **The Assumption of Mary** – body and soul into heaven.

5   **The Crowning of the Blessed Virgin Mary** – as queen of heaven.

THE LUMINOUS MYSTERIES

1   The Baptism of Jesus in the river Jordan – by his cousin John the Baptist.

2   The Wedding Feast of Cana – Jesus' first miracle, where he turns water into wine.

3   Jesus' Proclamation of the Kingdom of God – a phrase that occurs in the New Testament almost 100 times.

4   The Transfiguration – when Jesus goes up on a mountain and meets Moses and Elijah, the only Old Testament figures described as already in heaven, and is greeted by God as his son.

5   The Institution of the Eucharist – at the Last Supper.

The Rosary remains a popular devotion and many parish churches set aside a time or times in the weekly calendar when Catholics can gather there to say the Rosary together. Acknowledging a decline in interest in the Rosary among younger Catholics, Pope John Paul II, in 2002 in *Rosarium Virginis Mariae*, urged all, especially families, to return to this devotion:

> The Rosary of the Virgin Mary, which gradually took form in the second millennium under the guidance of the Spirit of God, is a prayer loved by countless saints and encouraged by the *magisterium*. Simple yet profound, it still remains, at the dawn of this third millennium, a prayer of great significance, destined to bring forth a harvest of holiness. It blends easily into the spiritual journey of the Christian life, which, after 2,000 years, has lost none of the freshness of its beginnings and feels drawn by the Spirit of God to 'set out into the deep' in order once more to proclaim, and even cry out, before the world that Jesus Christ is Lord and Saviour, 'the way, and the truth and the life', 'the goal of human history and the point on which the desires of history and civilization turn'.

Benediction and Exposition of the Blessed Sacrament

On its own, the word 'benediction' is simply a plea for divine help, based on Jewish practice, but the form of benediction most often seen in Catholicism is Benediction of the Blessed Sacrament. This devotion, which dates back to the thirteenth century, involves the host being displayed on the altar in an elaborate monstrance – or container. The congregation sings and prays, both silently and together. They are, Catholicism teaches, in the real presence of Christ, found in the host, his body. The priest may also, as part of Benediction, process around the church, wrapped in a humeral veil or shawl, and holding the monstrance, surrounded by incense (fragrant smoke). Many of the hymns and prayers that are part of Benediction will make reference to the Virgin Mary. A popular one is 'O Salutaris Hostia'.

Like the Rosary, Benediction has declined in popularity but remains part of the weekly calendar of many parish churches. An alternative is Exposition of the Blessed Sacrament, often scheduled before or after the Mass. 'The Catholic Church', states the Catechism, 'has always offered and still offers to the sacrament of Eucharist the cult of adoration, not only during Mass, but also outside of it, reserving the consecrated hosts with the utmost care, exposing them to the solemn veneration of the faithful, and carrying them in procession.' From earliest times, Catholics have been encouraged to pray before the consecrated host, either placed on the altar in a monstrance, or seen through the open doors of the tabernacle.

The Angelus

A short traditional devotion, accompanied by the ringing of a bell, to recall Christ's incarnation as a human being, the Angelus remains part of the national culture of countries such as Italy and Ireland. In Italy, the main state television channel broadcasts the Pope saying the Angelus each Sunday at noon, while in Ireland both the state radio and TV channels include it in their daily schedules.

It takes its name from the opening line – Angelus Domini nuntiavit Mariae ('The Angel of the Lord declared unto Mary') – and consists of a series of statements and replies, followed by the recitation of the 'Hail Mary'. Its origins are disputed but are believed to lie in eleventh-century monasticism where three 'Hail Marys' would be said during the ringing of the evening bell. Its format was standardized in the seventeenth century. Traditionally, it is recited three times a day – at 6.00 a.m., noon and 6.00 p.m.

The daily broadcast of the Angelus by Irish state radio and television has come under pressure with the decline in churchgoing and scandal surrounding the abusive activities of some priests and nuns with children in their care. In 2009, however, after a national debate, it was retained, though in an updated format.

> 'If the angelus bell provides a moment of reflection in an otherwise raucous and anxious world, then, surely, in the words of George Harrison, let it be.'
> Irish writer Mary Kenny on the campaign to end the Angelus on TV in Ireland

Stations of the Cross

A ritual of prayer, readings and reflection, the Stations of the Cross recalls the final hours, or Passion, of Jesus Christ. It can take place outside – most notably around the Colosseum in Rome on Good Friday during the pontificate of Pope John Paul II – with worshippers moving between 14 depictions of Christ's final suffering and death. Since the times of Saint Francis of Assisi, who encouraged the practice, most Catholic churches also include depictions of the 14 stations. It is most popular in the season of Lent, especially on Good Friday, the day when Christians believe Jesus was crucified.

The 14 stations are:

1 Jesus is condemned to death

2 Jesus receives the cross

3 Jesus falls the first time

4 Jesus meets his mother

5   Simon of Cyrene carries the cross

6   Saint Veronica wipes Jesus' face with her veil

7   Jesus falls the second time

8   Jesus meets the women of Jerusalem

9   Jesus falls the third time

10 Jesus is stripped of his garments

11 Crucifixion: Jesus is nailed to the cross

12 Jesus dies on the cross

13 Jesus' body is removed from the cross

14 Jesus is laid in the tomb.

There is a body of opinion within Catholicism that argues that a fifteenth station should be added – commemorating Jesus' resurrection.

The Divine Office

Based on the Jewish habit of praying at set hours of the day and night, the Divine Office was taken up by the Apostles and by the fourth century had become part of Catholic life, especially for priests and monks. It was considered too burdensome for the laity – requiring reading in a time of widespread illiteracy – and they were directed instead towards the Rosary. But the Second Vatican Council urged the benefits of the Divine Office on all Catholics.

Traditionally, the Divine Office divided the day into eight distinct times for prayer, reading and reflection, known as the canonical hours:

1   **Matins** – usually in the middle of the night

2   **Lauds** – at dawn

3   **Prime** – at 6 a.m.

4   **Terce** – at 9 a.m.

5 **Sext** – at midday

6 **None** – at 3 p.m.

7 **Vespers** – in the evening

8 **Compline** – night prayer before going to bed.

The Second Vatican Council, however, reduced the list from eight to seven, by incorporating Prime with Lauds.

At each of these stages of the day and night, Catholics turn to their breviary – a book of readings from the Bible, with particular emphasis on the Book of Psalms, prayers and chants. In some monastic communities, the Divine Office also includes singing.

Fasting and abstinence

Catholicism has fewer dietary laws than many other faiths. The best known of its practices is that of eating fish on Fridays. This was always a misrepresentation of the Church's position. Catholicism has long urged all members over the age of 14 to treat Fridays (except when they are Solemnities – feast days such as the Annunciation, the Assumption or All Saints' Day) as days of abstinence. On such days, they should avoid eating meat. In the past it was assumed that fish was the only alternative, but there are many dishes that can be eaten without meat in them.

These days of abstinence are designed to afford Catholics an opportunity to atone for their sins, and to reflect on the sacrifice of Jesus on Good Friday by making a small sacrifice of their own.

Key idea

On Fridays Catholics are encouraged to avoid eating meat as a small sacrifice that recalls Jesus' sacrifice on the cross on Good Friday.

Until 1966, the laws of abstinence were strictly followed. However, in that year, Pope Paul VI issued new guidelines, maintaining the practice but devolving responsibility for who should take part, and how other devotions might be substituted for abstinence, to local bishops' conferences and to Catholics' own consciences. In some countries, Catholics are encouraged to find time on Fridays to offer some sort of support to the needy in their community, rather than abstain from meat.

Separate from the days of abstinence are periods of fasting where no food or drink is to be taken. These apply to all Catholics aged between 18 and 60 and require them on two days in the year – Good Friday and Ash Wednesday (the first day of the penitential season of Lent) – to fast by having only one meal a day (or two small meals). Previously, Catholics had treated the whole season of Lent, and often Advent (running up to Christmas), as times of fasting.

Today there is much greater emphasis on the individual renouncing an aspect of their daily life, which they choose, as a way of marking Lent. Any money saved by this is then given to charity. But abstinence and fasting still, the Church insists, have a role to play.

> 'Mortification aims at the liberation of man, who often finds himself, because of concupiscence, almost chained by his own senses. Through "corporal fasting" man regains strength, and the wound inflicted on the dignity of our nature by intemperance is cured by the medicine of a salutary abstinence.'
>
> Pope Paul VI in his 1966 Apostolic Constitution, *Paenitemini* ('On Penance')

There are older traditions of fasting in Catholicism. Many used to fast and do penance on the Ember Days – four sets of three days (usually a Wednesday, Friday and Saturday) spread out throughout the year in Advent, Lent, around Pentecost and in September. And within religious orders – especially enclosed communities – there remains an emphasis on fasting and abstinence. Especially within female orders, this has been linked to anorexia.

Spotlight

Though the requirement for Catholics to eat fish on Fridays never existed in precisely that form, and the discipline of fasting has been neglected in recent times, I am constantly surprised at how many canteens in schools, offices and public buildings still make a point of offering a fish alternative on Fridays.

Case study: Food, women and sinfulness

The link between food and the sinfulness of women in particular is made at the very start of the Bible, when Eve's desire for the apple – the fruit in the Garden of Eden that God had forbidden her and Adam to eat – brings about the destruction of Paradise. 'The woman saw that the tree was good to eat and pleasing to the eye, and that it was desirable for the knowledge that it could give. So she took some of its fruit and ate it' (Genesis 3:6).

In recent times, a particular field of study for researchers and academics has been what is called 'holy anorexia', where believers – again especially women – feel themselves called to stop eating by their Catholic faith. The case most often quoted from the Catholic canon is that of the medieval saint Catherine of Siena, who would eat only bread, raw herbs and water and starved herself to death. She is sometimes called the first anorexic, but Saint Margaret of Cortona (1247–97) has an earlier claim. She worked ceaselessly among the needy of her home city and wrote: 'I want to die of starvation to satiate the poor.'

Some of these medieval women saints refused all food other than the host at daily Eucharistic services. Saint Veronica Giuliani (1660–1727) was denying herself food when she developed stigmata – the marks of the crucified Christ – on her body. The imprint of the crown of thorns, pressed on to Jesus on his way to Calvary, could reportedly be seen on her. The Carmelite Saint Mary Magdalene of Pazzi (1566–1607) was another who took up extreme fasting to show her solidarity with the poor.

Eucharistic fasting

Catholics used to be required to fast from midnight on the day before they received the Eucharist, as recognition of their spiritual hunger and thirst for Jesus. This was undertaken in imitation of Christ, who fasted for 40 days before beginning his public ministry. In the Beatitudes, set out in the Sermon on the Mount, Jesus said: 'Happy are those who hunger and thirst for what is right: they shall be satisfied' (Matthew 5:6).

However, in November 1964 Pope Paul VI reduced this period of fasting to one hour. The *Code of Canon Law* states: 'One who is to receive the Most Holy Eucharist is to abstain from any food or drink, with the exception of water and medicine, for at least the period of one hour before Holy Communion.'

The current rule allows for exceptions. If a priest celebrates more than one Mass on the same day, as often happens on Sunday, he is only bound to the one-hour fast before the first Mass. And those over the age of 60 or ill are exempt, though a 15-minute fast, if possible, is recommended.

These directives are not followed as rigorously as they once were. In 1980 Pope John Paul II lamented the fact in his Apostolic Letter *Dominicae Cenae* ('On the Mystery of the Eucharist'):

> What one finds most often is not so much a feeling of unworthiness as a certain lack of interior willingness, if one may use this expression, a lack of Eucharistic 'hunger' and 'thirst', which is also a sign of lack of adequate sensitivity towards the great sacrament of love and a lack of understanding of its nature.

Conclusion

The practice of individual Catholics may be changing faster than the relaxation by Rome of certain regulations over fasting and abstinence, but in the sacramental and devotional life of Catholicism there remains a bedrock of practice and belief that dates back to the earliest times of the Church. The Mass, the Eucharist and the sacraments are the very heart of what it means to be a Catholic.

Dig deeper

John Main, *Sacrament: The Christian Mystery* (Meditatio, 2014).

Timothy Radcliffe, *Stations of the Cross* (Liturgical Press, 2014).

Ruth Rees, *The Rosary: Space and Time* (Gracewing, 2004).

Lucy Russell (ed.), *Journeying with Jesus: Personal Reflections on the Stations of the Cross and Resurrection* (Bloomsbury, 2012).

Fact-check

1 How often is a Catholic obliged to attend Mass?
  a Daily
  b Weekly
  c Yearly
  d Never

2 Which of the following can a layperson *not* do during the Mass?
  a Read the lesson
  b Distribute communion
  c Stand on the altar
  d Read the gospel

3 How soon should Catholic parents baptise their newborn child?
  a As soon as possible
  b Within a month
  c Within three months
  d Within six months

4 Who baptised Jesus?
  a God
  b The Holy Spirit
  c His mother
  d John the Baptist

5 What does the white of a First Holy Communion dress symbolize?
  a Cleanliness
  b Purity
  c Godliness
  d Holiness

6 How many gifts of the Holy Spirit are received at confirmation?
  a 3
  b 5
  c 7
  d 21

7 In 2002 Pope John Paul II added ten new mysteries to the Rosary devotions. What are these known as?

   a Joyful

   b Sorrowful

   c Glorious

   d Luminous

8 How many beads are there on a typical rosary?

   a 10

   b 20

   c 30

   d 50

9 Which country continues to broadcast the Angelus bell on national state television on a daily basis?

   a Italy

   b Germany

   c Ireland

   d Brazil

10 How many Stations of the Cross are there?

   a 5

   b 10

   c 14

   d 18

The sacred and the secular

In this chapter you will learn:

▶ *where Catholic teaching clashes with secular orthodoxy*
▶ *how the annulment process works*
▶ *why abortion is such a key issue.*

All Christian denominations have a view of human sexuality that sits unhappily with many of the attitudes of modern, secular society. However, Catholicism enjoys a particular reputation for taking a conservative stance on a whole range of issues, from sex before marriage and homosexuality through to the appropriate response to the AIDS pandemic. Sometimes criticism of the Church is based on an out-dated perception of what it does actually teach. And even when that teaching is accurately conveyed before being attacked, the background to it is often not explained, leaving an impression that Catholicism is restrictive of sexual freedoms as a way of exercising control over Catholics' lives. While there may have been some truth in this assertion in medieval times – when Catholicism had ambitions to dominate every aspect of the lives of every person in Europe – in more recent times controversial Church rulings tend to spring from two sources:

1 a concern to direct humankind away from what the Church sees as potentially sinful behaviour that offends against God's law

2 a belief that the passing moral codes of any particular era need to be seen in the broader context of human history.

Catholics and sex

'My chief difficulties about the Church centre around her attitude to sex. So a case could evidently be made out for the Church being an alternative to sexual life. Whatever the truth is, it is certainly a fact of my own life that I have always had an either/or attitude about sex and the spiritual life.'
Convent-educated British novelist Antonia White in her *Diaries, 1926–57*

Catholics are forbidden to have sex before or outside marriage. This used also to be the prevailing behaviour code of Western society, shaped as it has been by Christian teaching. However, as secular attitudes to sexual behaviour have changed, and different choices have become generally acceptable, Catholicism has been left isolated in sticking to traditional notions of right and wrong in this area.

In times past, even in the most Church-dominated societies, there were of course always those who took no notice of Christian moral strictures about sexual relationships. However, back then, governments believed that marriage was the bedrock of a stable society and so tended to side with the Church in legislating on the basis of its teachings on the subject. Today's politicians, by contrast, place the emphasis more on the individual choice, and on the needs of the family, regardless of whether parents are married or living together, straight or gay. Governments' concerns have become essentially practical and pragmatic – how to create viable units as the building blocks of a stable society – rather than moral. And so the Church has often found itself at odds with secular legislators.

For Catholicism, when it comes to sex, as other questions, there remains the overarching moral dimension. The primary purpose of sex, it believes, is the procreation of children, and the correct context for creating children is within a marriage. So sex must be restricted to married, heterosexual couples.

Despite the Church's constant restatement of this position, it no longer appears to be one that is followed even by the majority of Catholics – especially in Western society, as the responses to the questionnaire sent out by the Vatican in advance of the October 2013 Synod on the Family demonstrated (see Chapter 2). Many will have several relationships before finding a life partner, and many will co habit before marriage, without ever feeling the need either to confess this in the sacrament of reconciliation or to stop going to the Eucharist as a result. The concept of 'living in sin', as it was once called, is no longer relevant to many Catholics. Some go further and resent the emphasis that Catholicism continues to place on what it regards as sexual sin, in contrast to other transgressions – economic and fiscal crimes, for instance – that will potentially impact on the lives of many more people.

Catholicism would answer that this emphasis on sex is found in equal measure in secular society. As the Vatican's 1975 *Declaration on Sexual Ethics* put it: 'In the present period, the corruption of morals has increased, and one of the most serious indications of this corruption is the unbridled exaltation of sex.'

Key idea

Catholicism teaches that every sexual act must be open to the transmission of human life and it regards all questions of sexual behaviour as moral matters, rather than issues of personal preference.

Catholicism was not the first religion or value system to regard sexual licence as dangerous. The Greek philosopher Plato (424–348 BC), for instance, taught that the human body was evil because it distracted the mind from the pursuit of truth. He saw sex as a function of the body. Aristotle (384–22 BC), his pupil, shared this view and regarded women as inferior to men and too ready to distract them with sex from cerebral matters. Both Aristotle and Plato were crucial in shaping Catholic thinking, most notably through Saint Thomas Aquinas who used their writings as the basis of his own highly influential teachings in the thirteenth century.

The resulting impression that Catholicism was hostile to sex has been hard to dispel, especially in the minds of those raised in the faith.

'The nuns wanted us to know that sex was something very powerful that you fooled with at your peril. They convinced us that our bodies were just charged with this amazing stuff and if we did so much as bare the top part of our arms, we could be an occasion of sin.'

Convent-educated writer Germaine Greer, in a 1991 essay

The Second Vatican Council did, however, make some inroads into the prevailing, essentially negative perception of sex held by Catholicism. In *Gaudium et Spes* (1965), it is stated: 'Married love is uniquely expressed and perfected by the exercise of the acts proper to marriage. Hence the acts in marriage by which the intimate and chaste union of all spouses take place are noble and honourable.'

Contraception

Catholicism, as we have already seen, reasserted its ban on artificial contraception in 1968, in the encyclical *Humanae Vitae*, on the grounds that the Pill, condoms and other devices interfered with the transmission of human life. The 'unitative' part – the pleasure – of sex cannot be separated, it said, from the 'procreative'.

This teaching has not been faithfully observed by many Catholics. The Church does, however, support other forms of 'natural' family planning. It thereby endorses the desire of many Catholic couples to limit the number of children they have – for economic, health and psychological reasons. It is a question of means. In his 1981 encyclical *Familiaris Consortio* ('On the Christian Family in the Modern World'), John Paul II wrote: 'The choice of the natural rhythms involves accepting the cycle of the person, that is, the woman, and thereby accepting dialogue, reciprocal respect, shared responsibility and self-control.'

However, some of the techniques Catholicism recommends – most of which involve identifying the times each month when the woman is fertile and abstaining from sex during those periods – are complicated and have lower success rates than 'artificial' means. And many would not accept any essential difference, in terms of purpose, between 'natural' and 'artificial' contraception.

Key idea

Catholics are forbidden to use any form of contraception that the Church deems 'artificial' – that is, the Pill, condoms or the cap.

Abortion

Human life begins, the Catholic Church teaches, at the moment the egg is fertilized by the sperm. From that moment forward, what medicine calls an embryo is, in Catholic eyes, an unborn child. Abortion is therefore the destruction of that life and a sin. This is a constant position that stretches back throughout the history of the Church. In *The City of God*, Saint Augustine (354–430) condemned those 'depraved married persons' who use poisons to 'stifle within the womb and eject the foetus that has been conceived… [They] do not deserve the name of husband and wife… it was not for wedlock but for fornication that they became united.'

Catholicism has been prominent in the campaign to prevent the legalization of abortion around the world and, where it already exists, to have it outlawed or access limited. Its efforts, though well supported and well reported, have achieved few successes with legislators, even in devoutly Catholic countries such as Italy and Ireland. While Catholicism does not support the antics of pro-life activists who direct violence towards abortion clinics and those who work in them, it does (in the Vatican's 1974 *Declaration on Procured Abortion*, for instance) attempt to portray abortion as part of a wider 'contraceptive mentality', where the ready availability of contraceptive pills creates a climate in which, if those pills fail to stop conception, recourse to abortion seems a natural step.

Key idea

Catholicism believes that human life begins at the moment of conception and therefore opposes all forms of abortion, regarding it as murder.

Some Catholic leaders also place the Church's stance on abortion within the context of its broader defence of human life. Cardinal Basil Hume (1923–99), leader of Catholics in England and Wales, stated on numerous occasions that to be pro-life was to demand not just an end to abortion but support for parents, decent homes, schools and hospitals, and job prospects for all. His counterpart in Scotland, Cardinal Thomas Winning (1925–2001), also demanded that Church opposition to abortion be matched by practical steps to offer real support, for example, in the form of housing, to women who were contemplating abortion because they could not face bringing a child into the world alone.

> **Spotlight**
>
> The Catholic authorities aren't always blind to the damage
> too literal an interpretation of the Church's teaching can do.
> Archbishop José Cardoso Sobrinho of Recife in Brazil attracted
> international headlines in 2009 when he excommunicated
> the doctors who had carried out an abortion on a nine-year-
> old girl raped by her stepfather. The girl's mother was also
> excommunicated, in line with Canon Law. Many Catholics,
> including senior churchmen, however, spoke out against the
> archbishop's actions and he was retired soon afterwards.

Assisted conception

Catholicism sees having children as one of the prime purposes
of marriage, and procreation as indivisibly linked with sex.
However, it warns Catholic couples against viewing having
children as a right, and teaches that children are a gift from God.

It bars couples struggling to have a child naturally from almost
all forms of assisted conception. With over 3 million children in
the world having been born through IVF (in vitro fertilization
techniques), according to statistics released in 2006, the
Church's opposition is another example of its setting its face
against secular society. The grounds for its opposition have
been presented many times, but are found with great clarity in
Donum Vitae ('The Gift of Life'), a 1987 document from the
Vatican's Congregation for the Doctrine of the Faith. It sets
out three principal objections to standard means of assisted
conception using in vitro fertilization methods:

1 That more than one egg at a time is fertilized outside the
wife's body by the husband's sperm, and that 'spare' embryos
created by this process may subsequently be destroyed or
used in experimentation (e.g. to generate stem-cells for
research). This contradicts the Church's teaching on the
dignity of human life, since, from the moment of conception,
the fertilized egg is regarded by Catholicism as a human life.

2 That artificial insemination and IVF separate sex and
procreation. 'Contraception deliberately deprives the conjugal

act of its openness to procreation... Homologous artificial fertilization, in seeking a procreation which is not the fruit of a specific act of conjugal union, objectively effects an analogous separation between the goods and the meanings of marriage.' So where *Humanae Vitae* says you cannot have sex without procreation, *Donum Vitae* argues, by association, that you cannot have procreation without sex.

3 That artificial insemination normally requires the husband to masturbate and that this is 'another sign of this dissociation' between sex and procreation. 'Even when it is done for the purposes of procreation, the act remains deprived of its unitative meaning. It lacks the sexual relationship called for by the moral order.'

There are forms of IVF that some Catholics believe do not offend against the laws of the Church – like aspects of the GIFT (gametes intra-fallopian transfer) technique, which can involve the simple act of transferring an egg from the woman's ovary to the lower end of her fallopian tube to overcome a blockage, after which conception can take place in the natural way.

Spotlight

The Church, in engaging in the debate over IVF, often stresses that having children should be seen as a gift, not a right. As with much of its teaching in this area, the logic of the statement may be clear, but try telling that to a couple desperate to have a child. Ideals and realities clash.

Homosexuality

'Although the particular inclination of the homosexual person is not a sin, it is more or less a strong tendency towards an intrinsic moral evil.'

Cardinal Joseph Ratzinger, later Pope Benedict XVI, in his 'Letter to the Bishops of the Catholic Church on the Pastoral Care of Homosexuals' (1986)

Though the New Testament contains condemnations of homosexuality from, among others, Saint Paul – 'men doing shameless things with men' (Romans 1:26–27) – it is not a subject that Jesus addresses, even though there would have been gay men and women among his audiences in that age, as in any other. Catholicism has, however, long maintained an absolute condemnation of homosexuality, listing it (alongside homicide, depriving workers of their pay, and oppressing widows and orphans) as one of four sins 'crying out to heaven for vengeance'.

In more recent times, though, with modern society discarding old prejudices against gays and lesbians, the Church has slowly adapted its position. It now condemns all discrimination and persecution of homosexuals. It also makes a distinction between 'orientation' – that is, being a man who is attracted sexually to other men, or a woman to other women – and giving 'expression' to that orientation – by having a sexual relationship. The second is 'intrinsically disordered', according to the Vatican's 1975 *Declaration on Sexual Ethics*, 'and can in no case be approved of', but the first is permissible, though it remains 'a serious depravity' and 'the sad consequence of rejecting God'.

Many openly gay Catholics, who continue to attend the sacraments, despite living in long-standing partnerships, would reply that they have not rejected God, but are, in fact, as God made them. Civil laws in European countries to permit civil partnerships between gay couples were denounced in 2003 by the Vatican as 'the legislation of evil'.

In July 2013, soon after his election, Pope Francis was challenged on the Church's teaching regarding homosexuality. 'If a person is gay and seeks God and has goodwill,' he replied, 'who am I to judge?' His softening of the Church's line was widely welcomed, as was his willingness to use the word 'gay'. He is believed to be the first pope to do so. Yet, the official teaching remains unchanged.

AIDS

> *'I ran up against young men dying of AIDS for whom God's love was such a necessity. Again and again my Church told them in the most violent terms known in the English language that their love was evil.'*
>
> Father Bernard Lynch, American Catholic priest and AIDS activist

When the AIDS pandemic began to make headlines in the 1980s, the Catholic Church's response was a limited one because it, like many others at the time, saw AIDS as something affecting only gay men. That belief has since been comprehensively disproved. The Church has subsequently stepped up its efforts to offer non-judgemental care and support for the many individuals and families around the world affected by HIV/AIDS.

Catholicism remains opposed, though, to the policies of international medical agencies, governments and the UN to encourage condom use as a way of preventing the transmission of AIDS. Catholicism's message is that abstinence outside marriage and fidelity within are the best ways of avoiding spreading infection.

It has even argued that a condom cannot be described as 'safe' because it may split. Cardinal Alfonso López Trujillo, President of the Vatican's Council for the Family, caused headlines in 2004 when he claimed that condoms, even when they did not split, offered inadequate protection against the transmission of the virus because they were permeable. His suggestions have subsequently been disproved by scientists.

Sexual abuse

In the 1990s Catholicism faced a rising tide of complaints about priests who had sexually abused children in their care over many decades. It was further shown that, even when the identity of some of these paedophile priests had been made known to Church authorities, they had simply been moved to other parishes and allowed to continue their abuse by bishops keen to keep such stories out of the newspapers. When some of the cases reached court – in Ireland, Australia, the United States, Canada, the United Kingdom and elsewhere – the Catholic Church was ordered to pay substantial damages. Even larger sums have been agreed in out-of-court settlements and some dioceses – especially in the United States – have faced financial ruin as a result.

In response to the revelations, the Vatican was largely silent until after the election of Pope Benedict XVI. He pressed local bishops' conferences to undertake root-and-branch reforms of their child protection procedures and introduce new guidelines, working closely with civil authorities to ensure that no such abuse or cover-up of that abuse could take place again. He removed the Vatican's protection from some prominent figures accused of abuse, who had taken refuge there under John Paul II, and he also met victims of clerical abuse.

Pope Francis has taken that process further, decreeing a 'zero-tolerance' approach to child abuse in the Church and establishing in December 2013 the Pontifical Commission for the Protection of Minors, which includes as members those who have been victims of abusive priests.

> 'Everything possible must be done to rid the Church of the scourge of the sexual abuse of minors and to open pathways of reconciliation and healing for those who were abused. Families need to know that the Church is making every effort to protect their children ... priority must not be given to any other kind of concern, whatever its nature, such as the desire to avoid scandal, since there is absolutely no place in ministry for those who abuse minors.'
>
> Pope Francis, *Letter to the Bishops of the World* (February 2015)

The revelations of abuse have done great damage to the reputation of Catholicism and to the trust traditionally placed in its priests, the vast majority of whom have had no part in such abuse. It has also prompted a new focus on vetting procedures in seminaries, with a view to picking out potential abusers at an early stage, and on the ongoing training and evaluation of priests and deacons, so as to spot and act on any warning signs of inappropriate behaviour.

Annulment

The Church's belief that marriage is for life is based on Jesus' words in Matthew's gospel: '…that is why a man must leave father and mother, and cling to his wife, and the two become one body. They are no longer two, therefore, but one body. So then, what God has united, man must not divide.'

Civil divorce is not recognized by Catholicism and, though obtaining a civil divorce does not bar either husband or wife from the sacraments, if either partner subsequently remarries in a civil service, he or she can be barred. To avoid this scenario, the Church offers the annulment procedure.

Unlike civil divorce, which is based on the differences between the couple that make their marriage unsustainable, annulment seeks evidence that the marriage was null – that is, invalid – usually from the very start. To obtain an annulment, either partner in a Catholic marriage has to approach their local diocese, via their parish priest, and face a tribunal, which will examine if there are grounds for declaring that marriage null and void.

Key idea

Catholicism does not allow divorce but recognizes, in its annulment procedure, that some marriages fail.

The annulment tribunal has nothing to do with financial settlements and the custody of children, and concerns itself only with trying to ascertain if a Catholic marriage has ever existed. If it decides there are grounds for allowing an annulment, that decision must be verified by a second tribunal in another diocese in the same country. If the two agree, the parties to the original marriage are free to marry again in church. Though their marriage is declared null, the Church stresses that any children born of that marriage are not illegitimate.

If the two tribunals disagree, however, the case is referred to the Sacred Rota, Catholicism's central court in Rome, for a final decision. It is called the Rota – from the Latin for wheel – because originally the court sat in the round. While the bulk of its caseload concerns annulments, it also hears appeals on other aspects of Canon Law.

Grounds for declaring a marriage null include (as set out in the *Code of Canon Law*):

▶ insufficient or impaired use of reason during the marriage ceremony by either partner

▶ grave lack of judgement in making the decision to marry, including a misunderstanding of what marriage is about, or immature consent to it

▶ fraud – that one partner was intentionally deceived about the presence or absence of a quality in the other

▶ wilful exclusion of children – that one partner, either explicitly or implicitly, intended to refuse to have sex with a view to conceiving a child

▶ wilful exclusion of marital fidelity – that one partner married intending, either explicitly or implicitly, not to remain faithful

▶ impotence – that one partner was unable to have sex.

Spotlight

Many Catholics whose marriage has broken down do not wish, through the annulment process, to seek a declaration that their marriage was null. They desire the Church's understanding as to why it began with good intentions, love and commitment, but then ended. I have met many who continue to attend Mass but feel excluded from the Eucharist because they have separated or divorced, rejected annulment, and then found a new and satisfying loving relationship that may or may not have included a civil marriage.

Case study: The annulment boom

Pope Gregory VII allowed ecclesiastical court procedures to start annulling Catholic marriages in the eleventh century, but in recent times the numbers of those seeking such a judgement has risen to record levels. In part, this can be explained by the process being simplified from the 1970s onwards. In the United States, for example, the number of annulments granted annually soared from 338 in 1968, to 28,918 in 1974, and to 63,933 in 1991. But, under pressure from the Vatican to take a harder line, by 2007 that annual figure had fallen to 35,000. The vast majority – three-quarters – were granted on the grounds of immature or impaired consent.

According to 2012 figures released by the Vatican, the United States accounts for 49 per cent of all annulments granted by the Catholic Church worldwide, followed by Poland (6 per cent), and Italy and Brazil (5 per cent each). Africa, with around 15 per cent of the world's Catholics, has fewer than 1 per cent of the Church's declarations of nullity.

Some 15 per cent of Catholics who divorce in the United States then seek an annulment, while 5.8 per cent of all married Catholic couples include one partner who has been previously married and then annulled. In November 2014 the Pope dismissed a Church official for attempting to sell annulments in what he called 'a public scandal'. 'We have to be careful that the procedure does not become some kind of business,' he warned and proposed that a new system would allow no-cost annulments.

Conclusion

The Catholic Church's teachings about various aspects of sex, relationships and conception remain controversial and out of step with many of the beliefs of the rest of society. Many Catholics do not follow to the letter the Vatican's rulings on such matters. For those who do, there can be much pain in the seeming gap between the realities of their lives and the ideals of the Church. However, there is a clear logic to the Church's insistence that human life begins at the moment of conception and is an inviolable gift from God, which links many of the teachings in this area.

Dig deeper

Jason Berry, *Lead Us Not into Temptation: Catholic Priests and the Sexual Abuse of Children* (Doubleday, 1992).

Mary Kenny, *Abortion: The Whole Story* (Quartet, 1986).

Bernard Lynch, *If It Wasn't Love: Sex, Death and God* (Circle, 2012).

Kate Saunders and Peter Stanford, *Catholics and Sex* (Heinemann, 1992).

Fact-check

1 As what did the Second Vatican Council describe 'married love'?
   a Noble and honourable
   b Potentially sinful
   c Inferior to celibacy
   d A distraction from God

2 Why does the Catholic Church ban 'artificial' forms of contraception? Because
   a They don't work
   b They are harmful
   c They interfere with the transmission of human life
   d They are expensive

3 When does the Catholic Church say human life begins?
   a When a baby is born
   b When the foetus is 14 days old
   c When the foetus is 12 weeks old
   d At the moment of conception

4 In what circumstances does Catholicism teach that abortion is permissible?
   a None
   b When the woman has been raped
   c When the woman may suffer mental trauma
   d When the unborn child is severely disabled

5 For a married couple to have children is, Catholicism says,
   a A right
   b A blessing
   c A gift from God
   d A duty

6 According to the Church's rules, when can a gay Catholic attend the sacraments?
   a Never
   b If single and celibate
   c If in a long-term, loving relationship
   d If in a gay marriage

7 When faced with reports of clerical abuse, to whom or what is a Catholic's first duty, according to Pope Francis?

a The Church

b The avoidance of scandal

c The victim

d The perpetrator

8 When did the papacy first allow the annulment of marriages?

a In the first century

b In the eleventh century

c In the twentieth century

d In 2005

9 Which is the Roman court that oversees the whole annulment process?

a The Sacred Rota

b The Marriage Tribunal

c The Pontifical Court

d The Court of Appeal

10 On what grounds are most annulments granted?

a Impotence

b Infidelity

c Inability to have children

d Immature or impaired consent

Dissent and dispute

In this chapter you will learn:

▶ *about the role of conscience in Catholicism*
▶ *about Church suspicion of mystics*
▶ *how liberation theology developed.*

The paramount role in a Catholic's life of a well-informed conscience has been a key part of the Church's moral teaching for centuries. Personal conscience, according to Saint Thomas Aquinas in the thirteenth century, should be the ultimate guide in all moral questions. It was, he said, the medium through which a human being received God's directives. He placed the dictate of conscience above any rules laid out by a human authority – including ecclesiastical ones.

Conscience

'Deep within his conscience, man discovers a law which he has not laid upon himself but which he must obey. Its voice, ever calling him to love and to do what is good and to avoid evil, tells him inwardly at the right moment: do this, shun that. For man has in his heart a law inscribed by God. His dignity lies in observing this law, and by it he will be judged.'

Gaudium et Spes (1965)

The Second Vatican Council, in its declaration on religious liberty, *Dignitatis Humanae* (1965), upheld the primacy of conscience:

> In all his activity, a man is bound to follow his conscience in order that he may come to God, the end and purpose of life. It follows that he is not to be forced to act in a manner contrary to his conscience. Nor, on the other hand, is he to be restrained from acting in accordance with his conscience, especially in matters religious.

However, the Council made an important distinction in this regard between infallible and non-infallible teachings:

> A Catholic who feels compelled to dissent ... from infallible teaching ... has no option but to sever his connection with the Church. On the other hand, when the question at issue is the obligatory force of non-definitive teaching ... then Catholics may dissent from such teaching for serious conscientious reasons and still consider themselves to be in full communion with the Church.

The question of conscience and the role of loyal dissent remains a delicate one in modern Catholicism. Pope John Paul II, in his message for World Peace Day in 1999, stressed once again the primacy of conscience: 'People are obliged to follow their conscience in all circumstances and cannot be forced to act against it.' Yet, there were those who felt that sometimes such words were directed more at the situation of religious believers who live in lands where the government wishes to clamp down on their freedom to worship. When it comes to dissent within the Church, Catholicism does place practical limits on freedom of conscience.

Key idea

The Church upholds the right of every believer to follow his or her conscience, regardless of Catholic teaching, but insists as well that conscience must be properly informed by those teachings.

The Internal Forum

There was a lively debate in Catholicism during the papacy of Pope John Paul II about the wide application of what, in Canon Law, is called the 'Internal Forum'. This concept falls short of the Protestant idea that each individual believer must right his or her conscience via his or her personal relationship with God. Catholicism still insists on an intermediary role for the priest between believer and God. But in this wider interpretation of the Internal Forum, a priest in the sacrament of reconciliation would not require a Catholic whose life fell short of the Church's ideals – someone living in a stable gay relationship, for instance, or who had remarried outside the Church without seeking an annulment – to promise to change those life circumstances before he or she received absolution. The Internal Forum was seen as a way of avoiding large numbers of otherwise faithful Catholics feeling that they were excluded from the Eucharist.

The concept was based on canon 130 of the 1983 *Code of Canon Law*: 'Of itself, the power of governance is exercised by the External Forum; sometimes, however, it is exercised by the Internal Forum only, but in such a way that the effects which its exercise is designed to have in the External Forum are not acknowledged in that forum, except in so far as the law prescribes this for determinate cases.' Essentially, this approach allows Catholics whose lives are publicly regarded as sinful by the Church – that is, in the External Forum – to reach a private accommodation with their own consciences and their priest, in the Internal Forum.

Many priests regarded it as an overly legal formula for routine pastoral sensitivity. However, Pope Benedict XVI, when he was still Cardinal Joseph Ratzinger, dismissed such a legal formula in 1991, saying that making exceptions for individuals in difficult situations might lead the faithful collectively 'into error and confusion regarding the Church's teaching'. He referred to 'numerous abuses committed under the rubric of the Internal Forum solution'. Yet with the Church's adherence to 'the seal of the confessional', it is impossible for the authorities to police any priest's decision to grant absolution during the sacrament of reconciliation.

Spotlight

Cardinal Ratzinger's tough words on the working of the Internal Forum seemed, to many, to have shut off that 'official' avenue for the exercise of conscience within the institutional Church.

Dissent

Some Catholic historians and theologians would argue that their Church has developed, grown and sustained itself for 2,000 years only because it has encountered dissent from within its ranks. Those voices that have questioned Church teaching have often been the ones that have pointed a way forward in the development of doctrine, though in their lifetimes they may well have been silenced or ignored. One frequently quoted example is that of Cardinal Newman, the English Anglican who converted to Catholicism in the middle years of the nineteenth century, amid a great storm of interest. In his lifetime, Newman often found his ideas treated with suspicion by his new Church, but in the century after his death he was considered one of the inspirations of the Second Vatican Council.

Spotlight

For those Catholics who fear that their dissent, or exercise of conscience, may put them at odds with their Church, the beatification of Cardinal Newman in 2010 – the first step towards him being named a saint – came as a great encouragement. His 'cause' had been many years in going through the Vatican's system.

Another group sometimes regarded as prophets without honour in their own Church, at least in their lifetimes, are Catholic mystics. The Church has been cautious about accepting reports of individuals having mystical visions of God, whether they be medieval nuns or nineteenth-century peasant girls who say they have seen the Virgin Mary.

Five Catholic mystics

Saint Bernard of Clairvaux (1098–1153) is perhaps best remembered today as a reformer of the monastic movement who inspired the Cistercian order, but his personal asceticism, his total disregard for any of the trappings and comforts of life, as well as his conviction that he was speaking God's truth, even when powerful figures in the Church did not want to hear it, made him many enemies. One cardinal dismissed him as 'that noisy and troublesome frog'. However, his mystical writings remain popular to this day.

Mechthild of Magdeburg (1207–82) was a German nun who recorded her visions of God, in exuberant and emotional language, in *The Flowing Light of the Godhead*. Her claim to theological insight and the criticisms she made, as a result of it, against Church leaders made her a controversial figure in her lifetime and she was forced in her final years to take refuge in a Cistercian nunnery at Helfta. Despite the enduring popularity of her mystical writings, the Church has refused all appeals to canonize her.

Thomas à Kempis (1380–1471) was a German-born monk, linked with a school of Rhineland mystics. He was a respected scholar in his lifetime, producing many admired commentaries on the Bible. His most enduring work, though, was *Imitation of Christ*, a meditation on the life and blessings of Jesus Christ. Many have pressed for his canonization, but his corpse was reputedly exhumed after his death, and splinters found behind his fingernails. It is said therefore that he was buried alive and tried to escape the afterlife, not appropriate behaviour, according to the Church, for a saint.

Saint John of the Cross (1542–91) was a Spanish Carmelite, poet and mystic, renowned for his co-operation with Teresa of Ávila in reforming their religious order, and for his mystical writings. His *Spiritual Canticle* – where the soul is the bride and Jesus the bridegroom – was written in 1578 when he was in prison and being flogged in public every week by opponents of his reforms. His *Dark Night of the Soul*, an account of the journey of a soul from body to union with God, is a classic of mystical literature.

Saint Pio of Pietrelcina (1887–1968), an Italian mystic, better known as Padre Pio, was a controversial figure in his lifetime on account of his claims of experiencing heavenly visions and ecstasies, the miraculous cures reportedly made through his intervention, and the stigmata he bore on his body – the marks of Christ's crucifixion. Senior Vatican officials dismissed him in the 1930s as insane, immoral and as using acid to produce his distinctive markings, but by the time of his death he was treated with respect by the Church and canonized by John Paul II in 2002.

Excommunication

Catholicism has, in the past, employed excommunication – literally exclusion from communion – as a weapon against those within its ranks who challenge papal or episcopal authority. Its use had become so commonplace by the time of the Reformation that the Council of Trent (1545–63) insisted on a slow-down. It ruled:

Although the sword of excommunication is the very sinews of ecclesiastical discipline and very salutary for keeping the people to the observance of their duty, yet it is to be used with sobriety and great circumspection; seeing that experience teaches that if it be wielded rashly or for slight causes, it is more despised than feared, and works more evil than good. Wherefore, such excommunications which are wont to be issued for the purpose of provoking a revelation, or on account of things lost or stolen, shall be issued by no one whomsoever but the bishop; and not then, except on account of some uncommon circumstance which moves the bishop thereunto, and after the matter has been by him diligently and very maturely weighed.

Since then, this has largely been the practice of Catholicism. Until recently a distinction was made between major and minor excommunication – the latter a bar placed on individuals from attending the sacraments, as a way of encouraging them to repent. However, this has now been abandoned. Such excommunications as there are – and they are extremely few – tend to be of public figures, such as the opponent of the Second Vatican Council, Archbishop Marcel Lefebvre, rather than of private individuals.

Key idea

Excommunication is the ultimate sanction that the Church can apply to a member. Its use is extremely rare.

Based on an ancient Jewish tradition of banning miscreants from the synagogue, excommunication is intended by Catholicism to have a healing power. Since you have to have been baptised to be excommunicated, it might be seen as a means of bringing individuals up short and forcing them to reconsider the actions that have brought them into dispute with the Church. Equally, since the sacrament of baptism can never be undone, the door always remains open for the excommunicated to return to the fold.

The power to excommunicate belongs to popes, cardinals and bishops, but the *Code of Canon Law* also sets out the grounds for *latae sententiae*, or automatic, excommunication. By certain actions, Catholics can incur excommunication even if it is never pronounced by a pope, cardinal or bishop. The onus is placed on the individual to confess their sins, repent and seek absolution. Among 'sins' that incur *latae sententiae* excommunication are:

▶ apostasy (canon 1364)

▶ heresy (canon 1364)

▶ schism (canon 1364)

▶ desecration of the Eucharist (canon 1367)

▶ physical violence against the Pope (canon 1370)

▶ ordination of a bishop without papal approval (canon 1382)

▶ procurement of a completed abortion (canon 1398).

Liberation theology

High on any list of movements of dissent within modern Catholicism would be the theology of liberation, which grew as both an academic and a popular practical expression of Catholicism in Latin America and Asia in the years after the Second Vatican Council. Its 'preferential option for the poor', endorsed at meetings of Latin American bishops in, first, Medellin in 1968 and then Puebla in 1979, was regarded with suspicion by Pope John Paul II and the then Cardinal Joseph Ratzinger, later Pope Benedict XVI. They repeatedly condemned what they saw as Marxist influence in liberation theology and imposed periods of silence on some of its best-known proponents.

One of those was the Brazilian friar Leonardo Boff. With his priest brother, Clodovis, he wrote the following question and answer sequence:

Q: How are we to be Christians in a world of destitution and injustice?

A: There can be only one answer: we can be followers of Jesus and true Christians only by making common cause with the poor and working out the gospel of liberation.

Liberation theology, which continues to thrive in Latin America and some areas of Asian Catholicism to this day, takes the example of Jesus' demand for social justice and uses it to insist on an improvement in the lives of the poor. In pursuit of that, some priests became involved in politics and trade unions – most notably four clerics who were members of Nicaragua's Sandinista government in the 1980s, who were rebuked in public by the Pope for their actions.

John Paul's attitude was, however, ambiguous. He was at one with the liberation theologians in demanding a more equal distribution of the world's goods between rich and poor. At Puebla, though, he warned, 'This conception of Christ as a political figure, a revolutionary, as the subversive of Nazareth, does not tally with the Church's catechism.' In 1984 and 1986 the Church issued major documents on liberation theology. They echoed John Paul's view that the Church should work for the liberation of the poor, but do so in an appropriate way for a Church, inspired not by a political vision of a perfect world but by helping each human being to find their freedom by redemption from sin.

Case study: Pope Francis and liberation theology

As the first pontiff to come from Latin America, Pope Francis's attitude to liberation theology has been much debated. He certainly shares none of the hostility shown towards it by his two predecessors and has publicly welcomed back into the fold some of those liberation theologians who had been condemned by Rome, including Leonardo Boff and one of the four priests who had been in the Nicaraguan government.

Pope Francis appointed a new head of the Vatican's Congregation for the Doctrine of the Faith – the body that once issued the official condemnation liberation theology. He is Cardinal Gerhard Ludwig Müller and has described Pope Francis as 'not so much a liberation theologian in the academic sense', but added: 'as far as pastoral work is concerned, he has close ties with liberation theology's concerns. What we can learn from him is the insight that there is no pastoral work without profound theology and vice versa.'

In line with his key demand that Catholicism be a 'poor church, for the poor', something he practised himself while a bishop in Argentina, making a priority of working in parishes in the shanty towns of Buenos Aires, Pope Francis can often sound and act exactly like a liberation theologian. But there is a key distinction. While still a cardinal in Argentina he had helped develop a refined version of liberation theology. He was the author of a key document issued by Latin American bishops in Aparecida in Brazil in 2007. This put heavy emphasis on helping the poor but stopped short of endorsing Marxism or any kind of revolutionary violence. 'We pledge to work harder so that our Latin American and Caribbean Church may continue to accompany our poorest brothers on their journey, even to martyrdom.'

Four leading Liberation theologians

Father Gustavo Gutiérrez (b.1928): A Peruvian theologian and Dominican priest who has spent his adult life working with the poor of Lima, Gutiérrez is regarded as the founding father of liberation theology. His book *A Theology of Liberation: History, Politics, Salvation* was published in 1971 and is the standard textbook of liberation theology.

Father Leonardo Boff (b.1938): A Brazilian theologian, philosopher and writer, he was summoned to Rome in 1985 and ordered to endure a year's silence after the Vatican objected to his book *Church: Charism and Power*. In 1992 he was facing another period of silence because Rome wished to avoid his involvement in the 'Earth Summit' in Rio de Janeiro where he teaches, but he decided to leave the priesthood.

Father Tissa Balasuriya (1924–2013): A Sri Lankan priest closely associated with the spread of liberation theology in Asia, he was excommunicated by the Vatican in 1997, on account of his writings, but the following year this was rescinded.

Archbishop Hélder Câmara (1909–99): A forerunner of the liberation theologians and an outspoken opponent of Brazil's authoritarian governments, he is best remembered for his remark:

'When I give food to the poor, they call me a saint. When I ask why they have no food, they call me a communist.' On his retirement, the Vatican replaced him in his archdiocese of Olinda and Recife with a conservative cleric who undid much of the Church social justice network that had been established there.

The Devil

'In the 1960s a new theological lobby was born that said the Devil did not exist. But God told us that the Devil exists. How can we deny this?'
Mgr Corrado Balducci, Vatican exorcist, speaking in 1995

Christianity was not the first religion to believe in an evil spirit, or devil, as a counter-force to God in the world. The origins of the idea of a cosmic battle between good and evil can be traced back through Judaism to Zoroastrianism in ancient Persia in the sixth century BC. However, it was Christianity, and Catholicism in particular, that took the idea of an evil spirit, a face to put to the otherwise intangible reality of evil, and made the figure of the Devil a haunting one in the mind of believers.

In the New Testament, it is the Devil who tries to tempt Jesus away from his divinely ordained mission, and in life, Catholicism taught, particularly in the medieval period, it is the Devil who waits at every turn to woo the faithful away from the path of righteousness into sin and ultimately damnation in hell. In medieval churches, the most prominent image was often that of the harrowing of hell, showing souls caught up in flames and eternal torment.

The last major Church document to deal at length with the Devil came at the Fourth Lateran Council in 1215. In more recent times, Catholicism has spoken rarely on the subject. The *Catechism of the Catholic Church*, published in 1993, makes no more than cursory mentions of the Devil, as the 'seductive voice' which lures Adam and Eve in the Garden of Eden, and more generally as a dangerous but ultimately insignificant force compared to God. Catholicism teaches that, come Judgement Day, there is only final defeat for the Devil to look forward to. His fate is already sealed, according to the Book of Revelation, the final chapter in the Bible. Until that Judgement Day, when Christ will return to earth in triumph, the Devil is left snapping at humanity's heels. 'He can impede but not stop the building of God's kingdom.'

Catholicism has, in its few recent pronouncements on the Devil, moved away from the notion of the Devil as a personality and towards the concept of him as a symbol of evil. 'What are the greatest needs of the Church today?' Pope Paul VI asked rhetorically in November 1972. 'Do not let our answer surprise you as being over-simple or even superstitious and unreal: one of the greatest needs is defence from that evil which is called the Devil.'

Key idea

The Devil as the embodiment of evil remains part of Catholic teaching, but is no longer so prominent a part of it as he was in the medieval period.

Exorcism

The downgrading of the Devil in Catholicism from the role he was given by the medieval Church has not been accompanied, however, by a parallel sidelining of the practice of exorcism. The Vatican maintains a network of priest exorcists in every diocese around the globe and continues to believe that, in rare cases, humans can suffer demonic possession.

In March 1982 Pope John Paul II was reported by the then Prefect of his household, Cardinal Jacques Martin, to have exorcized a young woman himself. Yet even senior exorcists, like Father Gabriel Amorth, who served under both John Paul and Benedict in the diocese of Rome, stress that in the vast majority of cases of those seeking exorcism, their problems can be dealt with more effectively by counselling.

The rites of exorcism used by the Catholic Church are based on Jesus' actions in casting out demons from possessed individuals in the gospels (Matthew 12:22–28). There are minor rites of exorcism in the wording of the baptismal service, for instance, or when a priest blesses a new home. The main rite of exorcism remains largely unchanged from that set out in 1614. In 1998 it was subject to minor revisions by the Vatican document *De Exorcismis et Supplicationibus Quibusdam* ('Of Exorcisms and Certain Supplications'). This presented a form of words to be used in Latin, but gave permission for local bishops' conferences to approve translations in local languages. It also approved for continuing use the traditional English prayer of exorcism:

> I command you, unclean spirit, whoever you are, along with all your minions now attacking this servant of God, by the mysteries of the incarnation, passion, resurrection and ascension of our Lord Jesus Christ, by the descent of the Holy Spirit, by the coming of our Lord for judgement, that you tell me by some sign your name, and the day and hour of your departure. I command you, moreover, to obey me to the letter, I who am a minister of God despite my unworthiness; nor shall you be emboldened to harm in any way this creature of God, or the bystanders, or any of their possessions. Depart, then, transgressor. Depart, seducer, full of lies and cunning, foe of virtue, persecutor of the innocent. Give place, abominable creature, give way, you monster, give way to Christ, in whom you found none of your works. For he has already stripped you of your powers and laid waste your kingdom, bound you prisoner and plundered your weapons. He has cast you forth into the outer darkness, where everlasting ruin awaits you and your abettors. You are guilty before his Son, our Lord Jesus Christ, whom you presumed to tempt, whom you dared to nail to the cross. You are guilty before the whole human race, to whom you proffered by your enticements the poisoned cup of death.

The rite of exorcism can only be performed by a priest after he has sought the permission of his bishop. It can include – as well as prayers – the laying on of hands, making the sign of the cross and sprinkling with holy water.

Key idea

Every Catholic diocese in the world has at least one priest who is also an exorcist.

Conclusion

Though Catholicism presents itself as an unchanging creed, it has over the centuries emphasized different aspects of its teachings. Its attitude to the Devil is a good example of how what was once a central feature of Catholic life has been downplayed in later centuries. Equally, what was once regarded as a dangerous, or even heretical, theological or practical approach can, again over time, become part of the mainstream. Change, development and refocusing are part of being a living Church.

Dig deeper

Sheridan Gilley, *Newman and His Age* (DLT, 1990).

Gustavo Gutiérrez, *A Theology of Liberation* (SCM, 2010).

Thomas à Kempis, *The Imitation of Christ* (Penguin, 2013).

Peter Stanford, *The Devil: A Biography* (Heinemann, 1996).

Fact-check

1 Which medieval mystic was once described by a cardinal as 'that noisy and troublesome frog'?
   a   Mechthild of Magdeburg
   b   Bernard of Clairvaux
   c   John of the Cross
   d   Saint Pio of Pietrelcina

2 Who wrote the spiritual classic *Imitation of Christ*?
   a   Thomas More
   b   Thomas à Becket
   c   Thomas à Kempis
   d   Thomas Aquinas

3 What are the marks of Christ's crucifixion called when they appear on a human body?
   a   Scars
   b   Stigmata
   c   Relics
   d   Shrouds

4 Which of the following is *not* among sins that can cause excommunication?
   a   Apostasy
   b   Heresy
   c   Schism
   d   Dissent

5 The 'preferential option for the poor' is a key concept in which one of the following?
   a   The *Code of Canon Law*
   b   The *Catechism*
   c   Dogmatic theology
   d   Liberation theology

6 In which Catholic country did four priests serve as government ministers in the 1980s?
   a   Italy
   b   Poland
   c   Nicaragua
   d   El Salvador

7 What did Pope John Paul II object to in liberation theology?
- **a** Its option for the poor
- **b** Its Latin American origins
- **c** Its Marxist analysis
- **d** Its economic theories

8 Who is widely regarded as the founding father of liberation theology?
- **a** Gustavo Gutiérrez
- **b** Leonardo Boff
- **c** Hélder Câmara
- **d** Oscar Romero

9 What does Catholicism say will happen to the Devil on Judgement Day?
- **a** He will be saved
- **b** He will be forgiven
- **c** He will be finally defeated
- **d** He will become an angel

10 Which of the following is part of the exorcism ritual?
- **a** Going to confession
- **b** Kneeling down
- **c** Sprinkling with holy water
- **d** Anointing with holy oil

Saints and martyrs

In this chapter you will learn:

▶ *how Catholicism makes saints*
▶ *about the role of miracles*
▶ *why martyrs are not always saints.*

The Catholic Church has long realized the value of role models in guiding believers towards good and moral lives. Throughout its history it has created saints to whom Catholics can turn in prayer for inspiration, strength and succour in times of trouble. Some saints are associated with particular needs – Saint Jude, for example, is traditionally associated with hopeless causes. In modern times, Pope John Paul II accelerated significantly the saint-making process and created during his 27-year pontificate more saints than had emerged in Catholicism during the past 500 years under his predecessors.

Canonization and beatification

Before 1234 the process of saint-making was carried out in Catholicism by popular acclaim. Individuals would be so esteemed after their death that their lives, or legends, would persist within the Church. This was particularly true of those who were martyred for their faith in the early years of Christianity. Stephen, a Jewish convert and deacon, is reported by the Acts of the Apostles (Chapters 6 and 7) to have been stoned to death because of his missionary work. He is regarded by Catholicism as the first martyr and the first saint. His powers as a preacher and miracle worker might be seen as setting the template for all subsequent saints.

However, this democratic system could be erratic. Often stories of different individuals would end up conflated. There is, for example, a clutch of early women saints (Pelagia, Apollinaris, Euphrosyne, Eugenia and Marina) who dressed as men to achieve ascetic lives and whose stories bear a remarkable similarity. And some early saints – Christopher, beloved of drivers, or Valentine, patron of lovers – are now thought never to have existed at all. Their biographies were based on earlier pagan gods, subsumed into the early Christian Church.

One of the earliest Catholic beliefs was in the 'communion of saints', reborn in heaven, marked out by their haloes (rings of light around their heads in traditional depictions) and acting as intermediaries between humanity and God. Hence individuals would have chosen for them a saint's name in baptism and later at confirmation would choose a saint as their guardian. There would be novenas – or sets of prayers to be recited regularly – to individual saints. The cult of the martyred dead became part of Christianity's promise of eternal life.

Key idea

Saints are guardians and role models for Catholics.

Haloes

The use of haloes in religious art predates Christianity. A ring of light above the head to mark out gods is seen in ancient Egyptian and Asian depictions, as well as in regard to Greek and Roman gods. Christianity first took up the practice around the fourth century, originally only for pictures of Jesus, but it quickly spread.

There is a hierarchy of haloes in Christian art. Triangular ones are reserved for the three persons of the Trinity – Father, Son and Holy Spirit. Round haloes, in white, gold or yellow, are for saints. The Virgin Mary has a circle of stars. A square halo would be used when depicting a living but saintly figure as, for example, in paintings of various popes. And Judas is traditionally given a black halo. Some artists would give Mary a mandorla, or all-body halo. The practice of depicting saints with haloes began to die out in the Renaissance period.

CENTRAL CONTROL OF SAINT-MAKING

As the leaders of the Church grew in their ambitions to regulate and orchestrate the lives of the faithful, the process of creating popular saints was also taken under control. In 1234 Pope Gregory IX published his *Decretals* – or collection of laws – in which he claimed for the Bishop of Rome absolute power over the causes of saints. As they were objects of devotion throughout the Church, he argued, only the Pope, with universal jurisdiction, could possess the authority to canonize (or make into a saint).

It is from this point onwards that the system still largely in operation in the Vatican today began to operate. The range of candidates elevated to sainthood became narrower, and greater proof was demanded, both of their virtues in life and of their intervention from beyond the grave.

Spotlight

Though popular acclaim is no longer a direct route to sainthood, the Vatican does take note of popular devotions. The French Carmelite Thérèse of Lisieux was unknown at the time of her death in 1897, but when her spiritual autobiography began to circulate, she won many admirers. During the World War I French soldiers would carry it with them to the trenches – and often to their graves. As her reputation grew, the Vatican stepped in effectively to endorse a popular movement when it canonized her in 1925.

Integral to the Catholic process of saint-making is the necessity for miracles. To become a saint, an individual, once dead, must be shown, to the satisfaction of the Church authorities (today the Congregation for the Causes of Saints), to have answered the prayers of the faithful for his or her intercession with God. The most straightforward 'proof' of this is that those praying to the would-be saint have then been miraculously cured. In the present system, proof of one miracle (the congregation employs doctors on its evaluation panel) is required for the candidate to be beatified – declared Blessed – and of two for them to be canonized – named a Saint.

Between 1234 and 1978 there were fewer than 300 successful candidates for the sainthood. The Church's habit was to ponder long and hard on its decisions, often taking more than 100 years to reach a verdict, and to promote only those of exceptional virtue.

John Paul II took a different approach. In one year alone (1988) he canonized 122 men and women. In total, he made 476 saints and approved 1,315 beatifications. The canonization or beatification ceremony of a local figure became a central part of his many trips around the world.

In making so many saints, he was keen to hold up to Catholics, and to the world, figures whom he believed embodied in their lives and achievements the essential Catholic values.

Inevitably, this meant that the length of time spent scrutinizing cases was shorter, and saints would be named soon after their deaths. The two most notable examples were Mother Teresa of Calcutta, who was beatified within six years of her death in 1997, and Monsignor Josemaría Escrivá, founder of the Opus Dei movement, canonized in 2002, 27 years after his death.

Case study: The canonization of Josemaría Escrivá

The beatification and then canonization of Josemaría Escrivá continues to be debated by Catholics as part of wider scrutiny of the Church's cumbersome and opaque saint-making process. Those in Opus Dei, the secretive movement Escrivá founded, defend his elevation to the sainthood, describing him as a model for all Catholics in his fidelity to the papacy, to Catholic teaching, and to promoting Catholic values in an often-hostile secular world.

It was this work that attracted the attention of Pope John Paul II. He saw Opus Dei as a vital ally in his fight against the expansion of secular values. He gave it the status of a personal prelature – answering only to him and not to the local bishop in the diocese where it operated. Others, though, worry about Monsignor Escrivá's legacy. One former leader of Spain's Catholic

Church, who had known him during this lifetime, described the beatification as 'a scandal'.

Meanwhile, Opus Dei itself has struggled to shake off the image it was given by Dan Brown's best-selling 2003 detective mystery, *The Da Vinci Code*, and the subsequent film, as a closed, fanatical organization, whose members indulge in excessive self-flagellation, and who are prepared even commit murder in order to protect its name. While the picture painted bears no resemblance to reality, some of Opus Dei's actual practices have been labelled by critics as 'cult-like'.

One contributing factor in the canonization of Monsignor Escrivá was the ability of Opus Dei to draw on its substantial financial resources to fund an accelerated progress for his 'cause' for sainthood through the various stages that the Vatican requires. Other religious organizations wanting to see their founders canonized have revealed that it can cost a six- or even seven-figure sum to fund the required documentation, bureaucracy, advocates and appearances before tribunals. They prefer to direct such resources to other more pressing needs.

Ten patron saints

1 **Alcoholics:** Saint Monica (322–87), mother of Saint Augustine, who was forced to endure a brutal marriage in the house of her unfriendly in-laws.
2 **Choirboys:** Saint Dominic Savio (1842–57), one of the youngest saints, a model student in his native Italy and an early co-worker of Saint John Bosco in founding the Salesian order, but died of lung disease.
3 **Foundry workers:** Saint Agatha (d.251), early Church virgin-martyr from southern Italy, credited with stopping an eruption of the volcano Mount Etna.
4 **Hairdressers:** Saint Martin de Porres (1579–1639), lived and worked with the poor in his native Peru, calling himself a 'poor slave', but in his youth had been apprenticed to a barber.
5 **Internet:** Saint Isidore of Seville (560–636), learned Spaniard who produced many books and an enduring encyclopedia.

6 **Lawyers:** Saint Thomas More (1478–1535), English lawyer who, though Henry VIII's chancellor, refused to sign his Oath of Supremacy out of loyalty to the Pope and was executed.

7 **Musicians:** Saint Cecilia (third century), high-born Christian convert and martyr, who reputedly survived three attempts to cut off her head and bequeathed her Roman house as a church. She is usually portrayed with a viola or at a small organ.

8 **Orphans:** Saint Jerome Emiliani (1481–1537), Venetian soldier who embraced Catholicism while in prison and set up three orphanages on his release.

9 **Rheumatism:** Saint James the Greater, one of the original 12 Apostles called by Jesus.

10 **Undertakers:** Saint Joseph of Arimathea, who offered his tomb to the Apostles as a place to bury Jesus after his crucifixion.

Modern martyrs

The close connection between martyrdom and sainthood was a feature of the early Church, and in more recent times the example of a number of figures who have died for their faith has continued to inspire Catholics, even if their causes for canonization have not always merited fast-tracking by the Vatican. Once an individual has been officially declared a martyr, however, it removes the requirement that a miracle be attributed to him or her before beatification can be granted. Proof of a miracle is, however, still required for canonization, though the Pope has the authority to dispense with this rule as well. Examples include:

▶ **Archbishop Oscar Romero** (1917–80): Archbishop of San Salvador for the last three years of his life, an outspoken opponent of the rulers of his country, and 'the voice of the voiceless', who spoke up for the mass of peasants who today already regard him as a saint. He was gunned down by soldiers at the altar as he said Mass in March 1980. The process for his beatification began under Pope John Paul II, but was delayed for many years until Pope Francis gave it his personal blessing in 2015 when he declared Romero a martyr.

▶ **Bishop Juan Gerardi** (1922–98): Survived one assassination attempt in 1980, but was killed soon after completing a report on human rights abuses in his native Guatemala. His murder was condemned by Pope John Paul II. Two soldiers were later convicted of the crime.

▶ The **seven monk-martyrs of Tibhirine:** In March 1996 Islamic fundamentalists, involved in a brutal conflict with the Algerian government, abducted seven French Cistercian monks from the monastery of Our Lady of Atlas, near Tibhirine. Seven weeks later they killed them.

Conclusion

The Vatican has now slowed the speed of canonizations once more, but the example of saints and martyrs remains central to Catholics' lives. The inspiration offered by figures from throughout the two millennia of the Church's history is a distinctive part of Catholicism's liturgies, prayers, literature and art.

Dig deeper

John Allen, *Opus Dei: Secrets and Power inside the Catholic Church* (Allen Lane, 2005).

Mary Craig, *Candles in the Dark: Six Modern Martyrs* (Hodder, 1986).

Francisco Goldman, *The Art of Political Murder: Who Killed Bishop Gerardi?* (Grove Atlantic, 2008).

Kenneth Woodward, *Making Saints: Inside the Vatican* (Chatto & Windus, 1991).

For more on Oscar Romero, go to www.romerotrust.org.uk

Fact-check

1 Which saint is associated with 'lost causes'?

   a   Judas

   b   Jude

   c   Jerome

   d   Justin

2 Who is regarded as the first Christian martyr?

   a   Paul

   b   Peter

   c   James

   d   Stephen

3 Triangular haloes in religious pictures are restricted to whom?

   a   The Virgin Mary

   b   The company of saints

   c   The Holy Trinity

   d   The Apostles

4 What is a mandorla?

   a   A musical instrument

   b   A tall candle

   c   The sign of the Holy Spirit

   d   An all-body halo

5 How many saints did Pope John Paul II create in 1988?

   a   5

   b   27

   c   75

   d   122

6 Who founded Opus Dei?

   a   Dan Brown

   b   Josemaría Escrivá

   c   Mother Teresa

   d   John of the Cross

7 How many miracles are required in most cases for canonization?

    a 1

    b 2

    c 3

    d None

8 Who is the patron saint of hairdressers?

    a Saint Carmen

    b Saint Martin de Porres

    c Saint Guy

    d Saint Vidal

9 Which instrument did Saint Cecilia, patron of musicians, play?

    a Guitar

    b Piano

    c Lute

    d Viola

10 How many years were there between Mother Teresa's death and her beatification?

    a 2

    b 6

    c 12

    d 25

Where two worlds overlap

In this chapter you will learn:

▶ *about the relationship of religion and science*
▶ *who are Catholic writers.*

The Second Vatican Council was all about encouraging a new relationship between Catholicism and the modern world, casting away old hostilities and the Church taking its place once more as a full participant in global affairs. This is largely what has followed, but such a level of engagement brings with it renewed scrutiny and fresh challenges.

In the political arena, the Church has found itself called on to make moral pronouncements on global conflicts and the arms race. The neutral position of Pius XII in World War II or Benedict XV in the Great War has been replaced by outspoken advocacy on the part of John Paul II, in particular of the fight for freedom from Soviet overlordship in eastern Europe. Age-old Catholic teaching about what constitutes a just war and how far each nation has the right to defend itself has been redefined in the light of contemporary contexts.

And in the broader social, cultural and scientific spheres of the modern world, Catholicism has found itself involved, discussed and criticized but, more crucially, also called upon to think afresh about traditional positions and new challenges.

Religion and science

The relationship between religion and science has long been a fraught one. Catholicism, in particular, has often resented and repressed the claims of scientists, though in more recent times a more productive dialogue has emerged, spearheaded by the Vatican's own Academy of Science.

Until the medieval period, Catholic thinkers believed that science should be a subsidiary branch of religion and worked to synthesize its discoveries with the teachings of the Church. That endeavour, however, became progressively more difficult and raised the issue that still stands at the heart of the dispute between religion and science – namely that they use very different methodologies. Catholicism is concerned with faith; science with proof. Most Catholics would say that they could not, empirically, prove the existence of God or Jesus' resurrection, but they believe in them. Most scientists would reply that their faith therefore is not soundly based.

🔑 Key idea

Religion and science haven't always been at odds, but theirs has long been a troubled relationship.

🔍 Case study: Father Athanasius Kircher

In the seventeenth century the German Jesuit Father Athanasius Kircher was widely celebrated across Europe for his books that combined scientific and spiritual discovery. 'Painter and poet say in vain, he's here,' reads the Latin inscription beneath the portrait that graced his books, 'his face and name are known throughout earth's sphere.' With the approval of his religious superiors and of the many senior clerics who were his friends, Father Kircher covered a dizzying range of subjects – geology, mathematics and magnetism. He invented, among other devices, a water-powered organ. In 1678 he opened the world's first public museum to show off the scientific discoveries he had made and the devices he had collected. He corresponded with Galileo, Newton and Descartes, taught Poussin perspective, and advised Bernini on the design of his *Fountain of the Four Rivers* in Rome's piazza Navona. Science, he believed, was the way to penetrate the workings of the Divine Mind. The human, the divine and the scientific came together as one.

In March 1638, when Mount Vesuvius was threatening to erupt, Father Kircher arrived in Naples and declared himself determined to see at first hand what was happening inside the volcano. He was lowered into its bubbling crater in a basket and lived to tell the tale in his next book. He wrote that he had had two purposes in mind as he descended into the noxious gases rising out of the crater. First, he had wanted to witness and record at first hand the geological changes in the Earth's core that were on show. And second, he had hoped to catch a glimpse of hell.

Galileo Galilei

> 'The intention of the Holy Spirit is to teach us how to go to heaven, not how the heavens go.'
>
> Galileo Galilei (1564–1642)

A measure of how and when the relationship between Catholicism and science first became fraught can be seen in the treatment of the Tuscan physicist, mathematician and astronomer, Galileo Galilei, today often called 'the father of modern science'. Galileo was a friend of popes and a Catholic, but attracted controversy because he spoke out publicly with the view that the earth revolved around a stationary sun. Catholicism, taking its lead from the Old Testament, officially rejected this position, though many senior figures accepted that Galileo was right.

In 1633 he was summoned before the Inquisition, forced to recant his views, and placed under house arrest for the remainder of his life. His writings were banned, until 1718, and remained on the Church's *Index of Forbidden Books* until 1835.

However, in 1992 Pope John Paul II, in the course of encouraging a new working relationship between religion and science, made a public statement of regret for the way in which the Church had treated Galileo.

As the Scientific Enlightenment, initiated by outstanding individuals like Galileo, gathered pace in the eighteenth century, Catholicism retreated ever more from any contact with science and was distrustful of its practitioners. When, in 1859, Charles Darwin published his *On the Origin of Species*, Catholicism could only condemn outright the idea that humanity was the product of an evolutionary process.

Darwin was not opposed to religion, but his conclusion – that humankind had evolved from animals – specifically rejected the creation account of the Book of Genesis. It also went against the mainstream view in Catholicism that animals and the whole environment had been created by God for the benefit of humankind.

However, in 1950, in *Humani Generis*, Pope Pius XII endorsed the first flickering of a rapprochement. He wrote that he did not forbid debate between Catholics and the scientific community on evolution and other associated matters. Others, like the French Jesuit and palaeontologist Father Pierre Teilhard de Chardin (1881–1955), were already working on a theology, in books like *The Phenomenon of Man*, that would bring together the theory of evolution with the account of the world's creation by God in the Book of Genesis. It is as a result of such work that Catholicism has refused to countenance such theories supported by evangelical Christians as creationism – that the world was literally made in seven days by God – or intelligent design (that God created matter and then worked through natural evolution).

Spotlight

Father Teilhard de Chardin is a classic example in Catholicism of the prophetic voice overlooked and silenced in his lifetime by the Church, but now regarded as a hero and regularly quoted by senior clerics with approval.

In 1996 Pope John Paul II all but gave Darwin his approval when he described evolution as 'no longer a mere hypothesis'. He went on: 'It is indeed remarkable that this theory [evolution] has been progressively accepted by researchers, following a series of discoveries in various fields of knowledge. The convergence, neither sought nor fabricated, of the results of the work that was conducted independently is in itself a significant argument in favour of this theory.'

Today the exchange between Catholicism and science takes place at many levels:

▶ In co-operation between clerics and psychiatrists and psychologists over those presenting themselves with what they describe as signs of demonic possession.

▶ Over research into infertility, where the Church opposes scientific work that creates 'spare embryos' (in Catholic eyes, human lives) for the purpose of research.

▶ In the Church urging scientists who wish to use stem cells in research to investigate the well-attested alternative sources of such cells, other than embryos.

▶ In the Church's own processes for scrutinizing claims of miraculous cures, made as a result of visits to shrines or in support of appeals to canonize individuals. The Church is assisted by a panel of scientists in examining such claims and seeking out any scientific explanation of what has occurred.

The Pontifical Academy of Science

Pius XI set up the Pontifical Academy of Science in 1936, in its current form, with the aim of promoting 'progress of the mathematical, physical and natural sciences, and the study of related epistemological questions and issues'. It works in six fields:

1 fundamental science

2 the science and technology of global questions and issues

3 science designed to assist the developing world

4 the ethics and politics of science

5 bioethics

6 epistemology (the theory of knowledge).

Around a third of its members at any time are Nobel laureates.

Spotlight

The Vatican has its own observatory. The *Specola Vaticana* is an astronomical research and educational institution. It has a laboratory at the Pope's summer residence in Castel Gandolfo, outside Rome, while the observatory is at Mount Graham in Arizona in the United States.

The 'just war'

In recent years, religion has often been held to lie at the base of all the conflicts in the world. No distinction is made, in making such charges, between good religion, faithful to the teachings and traditions of that faith, and bad religion, using erroneous or partial interpretations of its beliefs to suit a particular purpose.

In the New Testament, Jesus gives differing messages about whether it can ever be right to resort to violence to solve conflicts. In Matthew's gospel (5:39), he warns: 'I say this to you: offer the wicked man no resistance. On the contrary, if anyone hits you on the right cheek, offer the other as well.' But this pacifist impulse is checked (Luke 22:36) when he tells his followers: 'But now, if you have a purse take it; if you have a haversack, do the same; if you have no sword, sell your cloak and buy one.'

Saint Augustine was the first Catholic thinker to try to steer a course between these apparently opposite imperatives. He was reacting in the fourth century to the invasion of Rome and the need to defend the city against the barbarians. In *The City of God* he set out the 'just war' theory. It has remained at the heart of Catholicism ever since. The conditions for a just war are set out in the *Catechism*. It writes:

> The strict conditions for legitimate defence by military force require rigorous consideration. The gravity of such a decision makes it subject to rigorous conditions of moral legitimacy. At one and the same time:

- the damage inflicted by the aggressor on the nation or community of nations must be lasting, grave, and certain all other means of putting an end to it must have been shown to be impractical or ineffective

- there must be serious prospects of success

- the use of arms must not produce evils and disorders graver than the evil to be eliminated. The power of modern means of destruction weighs very heavily in evaluating this condition.

These are the traditional elements enumerated in what is called the 'just war' doctrine. The evaluation of these conditions for moral legitimacy belongs to the prudential judgement of those who have responsibility for the common good.

These are hard criteria to meet, and the presumption in modern Catholicism is against war. Particularly with the sophistication and power of modern weaponry, and the advent of nuclear arsenals with huge destructive power, some theologians would argue that it is now impossible for the criteria for a just war ever to be met.

Pope Paul VI appeared to share this view when in 1965, in his historic address to the United Nations, he appealed: 'war no more, war never again!' And, as if to emphasize the same point, Pope John Paul II condemned the first Gulf War in 1991 on no fewer than 56 separate occasions, while he described the 2003 invasion of Iraq as 'a defeat for humanity' with no justification morally or legally. As the United States and its allies toppled Saddam Hussein, John Paul reiterated his view that 'violence and arms can never resolve the problems of the world'.

On the wider question of the moral legitimacy of nuclear weapons, the Catholic Church has expressed its profound misgivings, but the Vatican has never condemned outright the policy of nuclear deterrence. Individual bishops' conferences around the world have, however, taken a more forthright stance, while individual Catholic clerics – like Monsignor Bruce Kent in Britain in the 1980s, as leader of the Campaign for Nuclear Disarmament – have demanded the scrapping of nuclear arsenals.

Key idea

While Catholicism holds in theory to the notion that a 'just war' is possible, modern weaponry has made the conditions necessary for that definition almost impossible in practice to achieve.

Catholicism and the arts

The Catholic Church has been one of the most significant patrons of the arts over the centuries and remains to this day custodian of some of the most outstanding buildings, paintings, frescoes and sculptures the world has ever seen. However, both the means by which some of these works of art were originally funded – the basilica of Saint Peter in Rome was paid for, in part, by the sale of indulgences, an abuse that was among the complaints of the Protestant reformers – and their ongoing custodianship remain controversial.

In modern times, as the Church has placed great emphasis on combating poverty and social justice, the suggestion is often heard that it should dispose of the great works of art it possesses to fund programmes to help the poor. Some bishops have tried to answer these pleas by, for example, selling their ornate palaces and moving into humbler homes among the poor of their dioceses. And the Vatican has attempted to turn its great repository for priceless treasures – the Vatican Museum – into a business whose profits go to support the work of the Church. This has been only partially successful. The operation of the Vatican and Curia still depends heavily on 'Peter's Pence', the annual offerings of Catholics around the world, made on the Feast of Saint Peter and Saint Paul (June 29).

While the days have long since gone when popes like Julius II (Pope 1503–13) could commission the greatest artists of the Renaissance – Bramante, Raphael and Michelangelo – to redesign and decorate the Vatican, Catholicism remains a noted patron of architects, makers of stained glass and fabric designers who, among others, assist in restoring, building and decorating churches and designing the vestments used in the liturgy. In the

Vatican's collection are, for instance, priests' vestments by the French artist Henri Matisse (1869–1954).

Among the most notable of modern Catholic churches and cathedrals are:

▶ **La Sagrada Familia** (in Catalan, 'The Holy Family') in Barcelona is the product of the faith and unique vision of Antoni Gaudí (1852–1926). Still being built and scheduled to be completed in 2026, it was to be, said the devout Catholic Gaudí, 'the last great sanctuary of Christendom'. Its irregular and fantastically intricate style owes something to art nouveau, but is impossible to categorize. Its Catholic symbolism is central to the whole vision. It has 18 towers of differing sizes, which represent the 12 Apostles, the four gospel writers, the Virgin Mary and – the tallest – Jesus Christ himself.

▶ **The cathedral of Our Lady of Aparecida,** in Brasília, was designed by Oscar Niemeyer (b.1907) in the 1950s as part of the new capital of Brazil. A pioneer in the use of reinforced concrete for building, Niemeyer created a striking white design shaped like two hands reaching upward to heaven.

▶ **The Metropolitan Cathedral of Christ the King,** Liverpool (known locally as 'Paddy's Wigwam'), stands on the site allocated to an earlier design by Edwin Lutyens (1869–1944) that would have rivalled St Peter's in Rome, but was deemed, in the austerity after World War II, to be too expensive. Frederick Gibberd's (1908–84) radical concrete and glass structure, with a central round tower of stained glass, has become a symbol of Liverpool since its consecration in 1967.

▶ **The basilica of Sacré-Cœur** (the 'Sacred Heart'), in Paris, stands on top of Montmartre, its white stone making it a feature of the city's skyline. Begun in Romano-Byzantine style in the 1870s, its construction was dogged by differences between the secular government of France and the Catholic Church. It was completed in 1914, long after architect Paul Abadie (1812–84) had died.

▶ **The basilica of Our Lady of Peace in** Yamoussoukro, the administrative capital of the West African state of Côte d'Ivoire, was built at the wish of the country's long-serving president, Félix Houphouët-Boigny (1905–93). It follows closely the design of St Peter's in Rome and is reputedly the largest Christian church in the world. Pope John Paul II consecrated it in 1990, but insisted that a hospital be built in its shadow.

The Catholic writer

> *'I am not a Catholic novelist. I am a novelist who happens to be a Catholic.'*
> French Nobel laureate François Mauriac (1885–1970)

The term 'Catholic writer' is a popular one, usually employed loosely to describe writers who are also Catholics and who touch on Catholic themes in their books. If strictly interpreted, however, the only ones who can truly claim to be 'Catholic writers' are those whose works receive the Imprimatur – or blessing – of their local bishop. This confirms that there are no errors in matters of faith in the text, and that it is therefore suitable reading for Catholics. However, imprimaturs are usually only sought for books of scholarship or theology.

The English novelist Graham Greene (1904–91), a convert to the Church in 1926, was often labelled a, if not *the*, Catholic writer. He disliked the term and rejected it. Instead, he described his faith as 'doubting my own doubts'. The phrase gives an indication of the themes he explored in his 'Catholic' novels. Those with the most profound exploration of Catholic themes include *Brighton Rock*, *The Heart of the Matter*, *The End of the Affair* and *The Power and the Glory*.

Other 'Catholic writers' include:

▶ **Gerard Manley Hopkins** (1844–89): Jesuit priest-poet, unpublished in his lifetime, he was a major influence on twentieth-century verse and mixes spiritual insights with acute observations of nature.

- **G.K. Chesterton** (1874–1936): British novelist, journalist and writer of Christian apologetics, he converted to Catholicism as an adult and is best remembered today for his Father Brown detective fiction.

- **Morris West** (1916–99): The Australian writer trained to be a Christian Brother for 12 years. He returned time and again in his writing to the clash of the sacred and the secular and the existence of evil within organizations set up to do good. His novel *The Shoes of the Fisherman* (1963) predicted the arrival 15 years later of the first Slavic pope.

- **Andrew Greeley** (1928–2013): An Irish-American priest, he has written a series of sexually explicit, best-selling romances, which include an undertow of theological debate. They include *The Cardinal Sins* (1981), and in 2004 he tackled the paedophile priest scandal in *Priestly Sin*.

Spotlight

It is sometimes argued that the age of the 'Catholic novel' ended with the Second Vatican Council. Catholic academic and novelist David Lodge chronicled the Council and the hopes it inspired among Catholics. 'I don't think that one can talk of the Catholic novel in quite such sharply defined terms any more, partly because Catholicism itself has become a much more confused – and confusing – faith, more difficult to define... the Church no longer presents that sort of monolithic, unified, uniform view of life which once it did.'

Modern Catholic movements

In addition to Opus Dei, several other recent Catholic movements, all supported enthusiastically by the papacy, have been established to meet the challenges of living a spiritual life in a secular society. Among them are:

- **Communion and Liberation** is a movement of lay people in Italy, though in recent years it has spread internationally. It defines its purpose as 'the education to Christian maturity of its adherents and collaboration in the mission of the Church in all the spheres of contemporary life'. Its founder was Father Luigi Giusanni (1922–2005), an Italian priest and schoolteacher. It has no form of membership, but encourages all who are interested to come along to weekly sessions known as 'Schools of Community'.

▶ **Focolare**, founded in northern Italy in 1943 by Chiara Lubich (1922–2008), has around 90,000 members worldwide, many of whom live in communities and take vows of celibacy. Its name comes from the Italian for 'family fireside' and its principal work is in the promotion of Christian unity.

Spotlight

Chiara Lubich was one of the most influential women in world Catholicism – and, in her quiet, understated way, one of the most inspiring. Focolare was inspired by Lubich's vision of living out gospel values in the world. It was, she said, 'one family united in truth', and, though a large proportion of those involved are Catholics, Focolare also embraces other Christians, people of other faiths, and those of none.

▶ **The Neo-Catechumenate** is dedicated to the renewal of the Church advocated by the Second Vatican Council. Founded in 1968 by Spanish painter and former atheist Kiko Argüello (b.1939), it tries to imitate the early Christian communities in its structures and dynamism. It has a particular interest in making converts from other faiths and numbers 13,500 small communities around the world, often based in parishes.

▶ **The Catholic Charismatic Renewal Movement** has close ties with charismatic movements in the Pentecostal and Evangelical Churches. It lays particular emphasis on vibrant worship, modern music and the role of the Holy Spirit. At charismatic services, the gifts of the Holy Spirit referred to in the New Testament are often in evidence, with people 'talking in tongues' (glossolalia – speaking in words that are apparently unintelligible), interpreting (what is being said in tongues) and healing. A development of the late 1960s, the movement represents another attempt to promote the ideals of the Second Vatican Council and was guided for many years by the prominent Council Father, Cardinal Leo-Josephus Suenens from Belgium (1904–96). It found particular inspiration in the words of *Lumen Gentium*: 'It is not only through the sacraments and the ministrations of the Church that the Holy Spirit makes holy the people, leads them and enriches them with his virtues... He also distributes special graces among the faithful of every rank. By these gifts he makes them fit and ready to undertake various tasks and offices for the renewal and building up of the Church.'

Conclusion

In meeting the challenge of the modern world, Catholics and their Church have taken many approaches, some very different from each other. What unites them is their loyalty to the papacy and their desire to ensure that Catholicism's message reaches even sceptical audiences and all those who could potentially benefit from it.

Dig deeper

Teilhard de Chardin, *The Phenomenon of Man* (Harper, 2008).

John Cornwell, *Powers of Darkness, Powers of Light* (Viking, 1991).

Stillman Drake, *Galileo: A Very Short Introduction* (Oxford University Press, 2001).

Joseph Pearce, *Literary Converts* (HarperCollins, 1999).

Fact-check

1 Which twentieth-century Jesuit tried to reconcile the theory of evolution with the story of God creating the world?
- **a** Ignatius Loyola
- **b** Pope Francis
- **c** Teilhard de Chardin
- **d** Gerard Manley Hopkins

2 When was the Pontifical Academy of Sciences established?
- **a** 1129
- **b** 1534
- **c** 1859
- **d** 1936

3 Where is the Vatican Observatory?
- **a** Rome
- **b** Naples
- **c** Arizona
- **d** Chile

4 Who first defined the 'just war' theory?
- **a** Jesus
- **b** Saint Paul
- **c** Saint Augustine
- **d** Thomas Aquinas

5 'War no more, war never again' were the words of which Pope when speaking to the United Nations?
- **a** John XXIII
- **b** Paul VI
- **c** John Paul II
- **d** Francis

6 On what feast day do Catholics make their annual offering for the upkeep of the Vatican?
- **a** Epiphany
- **b** Palm Sunday
- **c** Assumption
- **d** Saints Peter and Paul

7 Which architect designed Brasília's futuristic cathedral?
   a Oscar Niemeyer
   b Norman Foster
   c Edwin Lutyens
   d Le Corbusier

8 What do Liverpudlians call their modern Catholic cathedral?
   a Anfield
   b Paddy's Wigwam
   c Holy Trinity
   d The Mother Church

9 Who created the literary detective Father Brown?
   a Evelyn Waugh
   b Graham Greene
   c David Lodge
   d G.K. Chesterton

10 Among the gifts of the Holy Spirit, what is glossolalia?
   a Healing hands
   b Levitation
   c Speaking in tongues
   d Visions of the Virgin Mary

Conclusion:
One, Holy, Catholic
and Apostolic Church

The 1.229 billion Catholics in the world belong, in theory
and in the popular imagination, to a Church that is as wide-
ranging in its geographical spread as it is precise and united in
its teachings. Again, in theory, there is little room for regional
variations on the theme of what is laid down in a self-avowedly
hierarchical and non-democratic organization. The Pope, based
in the Vatican, has a unique and, according to Catholic doctrine,
sometimes infallible authority to teach, based on scripture and
the traditions of the Church. There should be, as Catholics state
in the Creed, just 'One, Holy, Catholic and Apostolic Church'.

One of the aspects of being a member of the Catholic Church
is that sense of being part of something so much bigger than
national or even continental boundaries. Catholicism manages
to distil down in its core beliefs something that has a power
to unite humankind around the globe. Attend a Mass in Addis
Ababa, the Amazon basin or Aldershot and in the Catholic
liturgy there is a familiarity that conveys that participants are
part of a global family.

Yet, it is a familiarity that cannot disguise that there are huge
economic, political and social differences between the world's
Catholics. These are inevitable in such a far-flung organization,
which stretches from the wealthy capitals of the developed
world to the favelas of South America and the shanty towns of
Africa, from presidents, prime ministers and kings to the most
needy and marginalized on the planet.

As a consequence, there are differences in emphasis as to what
it means to be a Catholic between individual believers, and
between believers in individual societies, which each have their
own priorities, history, culture, customs and baggage. English
Catholics, for instance, remain in some way shaped by the

experience of their Church being suppressed for almost 300 years following the Reformation.

More generally, there remains an undeniable gap between the ideals that the Church teaches and the reality of many Catholics' lives. Not every Catholic follows to the letter every teaching of the Church. The areas of divergence from those teachings, and the degree, will be wide-ranging and, sometimes, will appear to follow no obvious logic. So those who, for instance, prefer a 'traditional' Latin liturgy will often also be the ones pushing for the Church to take a more 'progressive' stance on social justice. And those who embrace a 'modern', free style of worship will, sometimes, be the ones who are defiantly 'un-modern' in their stance on matters of personal morality.

The reason for such disparity comes down in part to economics and politics – what is possible and desirable in different societies around the world – and in part to personal temperament and conscience. Catholics live their lives in the context of radically different societies that shape the daily reality of their faith.

Yet for all that, at core, there continues to be, after 2,000 years, a template of beliefs and liturgy at the heart of global Catholicism that unites more than it divides. And, as the symbol of that unity, Pope Francis, in the Vatican and on his travels, remains the visible sign of the Catholic Church.

Spotlight: Taking it further

Websites

The Catholic Faith Centre offers materials for those interested in Catholicism – www.catholicfaith.org.uk – or write to them c/o 39 Eccleston Square, London SW1V 1PL.

Face to face

The most direct route is to attend your local Catholic church and/or to make contact with your local priest. The Church runs a series of programmes in each parish and diocese for those interested in exploring the Catholic faith. If you feel nervous of face-to-face contact, there will be a range of booklets at the back of the church, along with copies of the vibrant national Catholic press.

Glossary

ANGELUS   A short, traditional set of prayers, performed several times daily, to remind Catholics of Jesus' incarnation on earth as both human and divine.

APOCRYPHA   The sacred books that have not been included by the Church in either the Old or New Testaments.

APOSTOLIC SUCCESSION   The belief in Catholicism that Jesus chose Saint Peter from among his Apostles to be the first leader and Pope of his church on earth, and that each Pope thereafter is linked via Peter to Christ.

BEATIFICATION   When the Church declares someone who has died to be 'Blessed'. This is done after an investigation of the person's life and is only awarded if that life is shown to have been one of exceptional faith. A further requirement is that the Church is satisfied that one miraculous cure has resulted from the intercession of that individual from beyond the grave. Beatification is a step on the path to canonization.

BENEDICTION   A short prayer for divine help, often part of a service.

CANONIZATION   When the Church declares someone a saint. The qualifications are the same as for beatification, but with one major difference: proof of two miracles is required.

CATECHISM   A rulebook for Catholics.

CHARISM   From the Greek for 'grace', the influence of the divine experienced as a gift within individuals.

COUNCIL OF TRENT   The key meeting, held intermittently in the Italian city of the same name between 1545 and 1563, when the Catholic Church formulated its response to the Reformation.

CURIA   The bureaucracy that serves the popes in Rome.

DIVINE OFFICE   A structure of prayers and readings to cover the whole day.

ENLIGHTENMENT   An eighteenth-century philosophical movement in Western Europe which rejected religious pessimism as to the sinfulness of humankind and preached instead optimism and the power of each human being to reach their potential on earth.

EUCHARIST   One of the seven sacraments, also known as Holy Communion.

EXTREME UNCTION   Meaning 'final anointing' and a traditional phrase for the sacrament given to those believed to be nearing death.

GENTILE   In the early Christian Church, and in the New Testament, Gentile is a term used to describe non-Jews.

HOLY   See Another phrase to describe the Vatican, derived from a phrase used in the enthronement ceremony of popes.

HOMILY   A commentary on scripture, usually given during the Mass.

ICONOCLASM   The destruction of religious icons, seen within the Orthodox Church in the eighth and ninth centuries.

IMPRIMATUR   The formal approval of the local bishop, given to a book or document produced by a priest or religious writer under his authority, and an indication that what is said or written fits with the teachings of the Catholic Church.

INDULGENCES   The full or partial remission of punishments or penances to be done in this life for sins committed against Church teaching and confessed to a priest.

JUDAISM   The faith and beliefs of Jews.

LITURGY   The form of words and music used by the Church for its services.

MAGISTERIUM   The teaching authority of the Church, usually vested in the person of the Pope.

MASS   The celebration of the Eucharist.

MENDICANT   From the Latin for 'to beg', this refers to monks and religious followers who rely exclusively on charity to survive.

OSTPOLITIK   The policy adopted by the Vatican, in the wake of the Second World War, of entering into constructive dialogue with communist regimes in eastern Europe that rejected religion.

PAPACY   The noun used to describe the office of the popes.

PATRIARCHATE   Refers to the ecclesiastical authority of patriarchs, senior figures in the early Church who rivalled the bishops of Rome.

ROSARY   A Catholic ritual, using beads, where a strict formula of prayers is repeated while individuals reflect on events in the life of the Virgin Mary.

SACRED ROTA   One of the highest appeal courts in the Catholic Church's system of Church (or Canon) Law.

SIMONY   The sin of paying for offices or positions in the hierarchy of the Church, named after Simon Magus, who appears in the Acts of the Apostles (8:18–24). Simon Magus offers the disciples, Peter and John, payment if anyone he places his hands on would then receive the power of the Holy Spirit.

SOLEMNITIES   A principal holy day in the Church's calendar.

SYNOD   A Church meeting, often of bishops and cardinals.

TRANSUBSTANTIATION   The Catholic belief that Jesus' body and blood are present in the bread and wine at Holy Communion in more than a purely symbolic way.

TRINITARIAN   Anything to do with the Holy Trinity, the three persons in one God: Father, Son and Holy Spirit.

TRINITY   The Christian belief that there are three persons in one God: God the Father, God the Son (Jesus) and God the Holy Spirit.

ULTRAMONTANISM   The belief that the Pope's powers override those of any local secular or Church figure. It literally means 'over the mountains' and refers to attempts to make the Pope's word as important in faraway countries as it was in Rome.

Answers to fact-checks

CHAPTER 1
1 c
2 d
3 b
4 d
5 c
6 b
7 a
8 a
9 d
10 c

CHAPTER 2
1 b
2 a
3 c
4 c
5 d
6 c
7 b
8 a
9 c
10 b

CHAPTER 3
1 c
2 a
3 d
4 b
5 d
6 c
7 a
8 c
9 d
10 c

CHAPTER 4
1 c
2 d
3 a
4 b
5 c
6 d
7 a
8 c
9 c
10 b

CHAPTER 5
1 b
2 d
3 c
4 d
5 a
6 b
7 d
8 a
9 c
10 b

CHAPTER 6
1 a
2 c
3 d
4 a
5 b
6 c
7 d
8 b
9 d
10 b

CHAPTER 7
1 c
2 d
3 a
4 d
5 c
6 a
7 b
8 b
9 c
10 d

CHAPTER 8
1 d
2 c
3 a
4 b
5 a
6 b
7 a
8 d
9 d
10 a

CHAPTER 9	CHAPTER 11	CHAPTER 13
1 c	1 a	1 b
2 a	2 c	2 d
3 c	3 d	3 c
4 b	4 a	4 d
5 c	5 c	5 d
6 a	6 b	6 b
7 d	7 c	7 b
8 c	8 b	8 b
9 b	9 a	9 d
10 d	10 d	10 b

CHAPTER 10	CHAPTER 12	CHAPTER 14
1 b	1 b	1 c
2 d	2 c	2 d
3 a	3 b	3 c
4 d	4 d	4 c
5 b	5 d	5 b
6 c	6 c	6 d
7 d	7 c	7 a
8 d	8 a	8 b
9 c	9 c	9 d
10 c	10 c	10 c

Index